W0404202

Freeway

Workbook – Allgemeine Ausgabe

Englisch für das Berufskolleg
Baden-Württemberg

von
Catherine Küpper
Wolfgang Rosenkranz (Hrsg.)
Graham Tucker

Ernst Klett Verlag
Stuttgart · Leipzig

Symbole und Verweise

- R Rezeption
- M Mediation
- P Produktion
- ► Verweis auf Grammar Files (Schülerbuch)
- ► Verweis auf Skills Files (Schülerbuch)

◎ A 3.17 Audioverweis mit Tracknummer

y6d6su 🌐 **Zusatzangebot im Internet:**
Dieser Freeway-Code führt zu den Audios im MP3-Format sowie zu den Lösungen. Geben Sie einfach den Code auf **www.klett.de** ein.

Vocabulary revision

1 People

Use the words in the box to fill in suitable pairs in the table below.

female – aunt – wife – women – son – dad – gentleman – life – grandchildren – child

1.	grandparents	
2.	men	
3.	daughter	
4.	adult	
5.	mum	
6.	husband	
7.	lady	
8.	male	
9.	uncle	
10.	death	

2 Jobs

Match the jobs on the left with a suitable description on the right by filling in the correct letter.

1.	a cook		a)	cares for sick people
2.	a farmer		b)	repairs machines
3.	a postman		c)	serves food and drinks in a restaurant
4.	a nursery school teacher		d)	prepares meals
5.	a landlady		e)	cuts and sells meat in a shop
6.	a mechanic		f)	rents rooms to other people
7.	a waiter		g)	cultivates land and raises animals
8.	a butcher		h)	sells goods in a shop
9.	a shop assistant		i)	cares for young children
10.	a nurse		j)	collects and delivers mail

3 Work

Fill in the corresponding English words.

ACROSS

2. Angestellte(r), Beschäftigter
3. Bewerber(in)
5. Karriere
8. Bewerbung
10. Hersteller, Produzent
11. verdienen
15. Wirtschaft

DOWN

1. Wettbewerb
4. Fabrik
6. Abteilung
7. Unternehmen
9. werben
12. Werkzeug
13. Käufer
14. Arbeit(splatz), Beruf

4 The home, rooms and furniture

Give the names of the parts of the house (numbers 1 and 2), the rooms (numbers 3 to 6) and the pieces of furniture (numbers 7 to 18).
Use a separate sheet of paper.

5 Traffic and transport

Use the endings in the box to create English words to do with traffic and transport. Then translate the words into German. If you are not sure, check the list of basic vocabulary in your student's book.

dent – ort – gage – cycle – ine – form – icle – ney – way – case – et –
ival – enger – toms – rol – go – ry – ght – eel – ver

	English word	German translation
1.	bi	
2.	airp	
3.	pass	
4.	acci	
5.	rail	
6.	plat	
7.	bag	
8.	car	
9.	veh	
10.	wh	

	English word	German translation
11.	dri	
12.	fli	
13.	eng	
14.	pet	
15.	tick	
16.	arr	
17.	suit	
18.	cus	
19.	jour	
20.	lor	

6 The body, clothes and accessories

Find words for the parts of the body, clothes and accessories. Use a separate sheet of paper.

7 At school

Match the words in the table below with their definitions and fill in the correct letter.

1.	teacher		**a)**	a child in school
2.	pupil		**b)**	a place where classes meet
3.	class		**c)**	a dark surface in a classroom for writing
4.	classroom		**d)**	task that a student is given to do at home
5.	classmate		**e)**	a piece of furniture that is like a table and is used for writing
6.	desk		**f)**	a person whose job it is to instruct students
7.	lesson		**g)**	group of students who meet at school regularly
8.	blackboard		**h)**	a white stick used for writing in class
9.	a piece of chalk		**i)**	a member of the same class
10.	homework		**j)**	a period of time when people are taught
11.	attend		**k)**	give lessons
12.	teach		**l)**	regularly go to (school)

8 Eating and drinking

Fill in the missing vowels. Then fill in the German meanings of the words.

Example: l_m_n = lemon - Zitrone

1.	l_nch	
2.	m_rm_l_d_	
3.	m_ _t	
4.	m_lk	
5.	p_t_t_	
6.	s_g_r	
7.	s_pp_r	
8.	d_nn_r	
9.	t_ _	
10.	t_m_t_	
11.	c_ff_ _	
12.	c_p	
13.	pl_t_	
14.	_gg	
15.	f_rk	

16.	v_g_t_bl_	
17.	w_n_	
18.	_ppl_	
19.	b_ttl_	
20.	br_ _d	
21.	br_ _kf_st	
22.	c_k_	
23.	ch_c_l_t_	
24.	ch_ _s_	
25.	ch_ps	
26.	sp_ _n	
27.	kn_f_	
28.	_c_ cr_ _m	
29.	sw_ _t	
30.	h_ngr_	

9 Using adjectives to describe people and things

Match the following German words in the list with their English equivalents in the box.

active – angry – beautiful – bored – boring – careful – careless – certain – clever – different – difficult – dirty – friendly – hungry – important – interesting – surprised – tired – unfriendly – unhappy

1.	interessant	
2.	langweilig	
3.	unterschiedlich, verschieden	
4.	müde	
5.	wütend	
6.	freundlich	
7.	aktiv	
8.	schön	
9.	schmutzig	
10.	hungrig	

11.	unfreundlich	
12.	gelangweilt	
13.	sicher, bestimmt, gewiss	
14.	überrascht	
15.	vorsichtig, sorgfältig	
16.	sorglos	
17.	schwierig	
18.	unglücklich	
19.	klug, schlau	
20.	wichtig	

10 What people do (verbs + prepositions and particles)

Complete the following sentences by filling in a suitable word from the box below.

about – after – down – for – for – from – off – on – on – on – over – to – up – with

1. The student applied __________ a part-time job.
2. She was looking __________ a job where she could work late in the afternoon.
3. First the student enquired __________ the company.
4. She listened carefully __________ what a friend said.
5. The company deals __________ all sorts of goods.
6. Their success depends __________ the quality of the goods.
7. Their products differ __________ products made by other companies.
8. In her job the student has to look __________ the customers' children.
9. She often sits __________ with the children and reads stories to them.
10. When she turns __________ the page she asks the children how they think the story will go __________.
11. The children put __________ their hands when they have an interesting idea.
12. After the children have left the room the student turns __________ the lights, puts __________ her coat and goes home.

11 Nature

Complete the following table by filling in the corresponding English words. Then you can read the solution from top to bottom.

1. Energie, Kraft
2. Pflanze
3. Fluss
4. Entfernung
5. Baum
6. Umweltverschmutzung
7. Dunkelheit
8. Atmosphäre
9. Meer
10. Sonnenschein
11. Wetter

Solution ▼

1.														
2.														
3.														
4.														
5.														
6.														
7.														
8.														
9.														
10.														
11.														

Grammar revision

1 Articles

a) **Fill in "a" or "an".** ► Indefinite article, p. 175

1.	a	student
2.	an	exercise
3.		address
4.		college

5.		examination
6.		university
7.		hour
8.		office

b) **Fill in "the" where necessary.** ► Definite article, p. 175

Visiting a friend in London

My English friend Derek goes to **[1.]** ______________ college. When I visited him he showed me **[2.]** ______________ college buildings. Next year he will attend **[3.]** ______________ university. Maybe he can study at **[4.]** ______________ University of Exeter. In my next holidays I will go to **[5.]** ______________ Great Britain. I will be in **[6.]** ______________ London and will see **[7.]** ______________ Thames and **[8.]** ______________ Buckingham Palace. I would like to fly to **[9.]** ______________ London Gatwick Airport. I hope that my friend can meet me at **[10.]** ______________ airport.

2 Irregular plural forms

a) **Complete the following list of singular and plural forms. Watch the spelling of the words!** ► Plural, p. 176

	Singular	Plural
1.	man	men
2.		universities
3.	address	
4.		women
5.	city	
6.	child	

	Singular	Plural
7.		lives
8.	foot	
9.		teeth
10.		yourselves
11.	copy	
12.	wife	

b) **Write the words from the box below under the correct headings. (Singular or Plural)**

information – **jeans** – weather – glasses *(Brille)* – homework – furniture – trousers – knowledge – mathematics – news – work – nature – clothes – advice – economics – hair

Singular		Plural	
information	is	jeans	are

3 Some or any?

► Some or any? p. 180

Fill in "some" or "any".

At the market

Customer: I'd like [1.] some red apples, please.

Salesperson: Here you are. Is there [2.] anything else I can do for you?

Customer: Yes, I can't see [3.] ____________ strawberries here. Have you got [4.] ____________?

Salesperson: Of course. We've got [5.] ____________ very sweet ones over here. Would you like [6.] ____________?

Customer: Oh yes. I love strawberries. And I mustn't forget to get [7.] ____________ bananas.

Salesperson: That's five pounds then.

Customer: Oh dear! I haven't got [8.] ____________ small change. Can you change a twenty-pound note?

Salesperson: No problem. That's fine.

4 Much – many – (a) little – (a) few

► Much – many – a lot of, p. 181 ► Little / a little – few / a few, p. 181

Fill in the following gaps with "much, many, a lot of, little, a little, few, a few".

Travelling in winter

During the winter only [1.] a few people stay at seaside hotels in southern England. There is not [2.] ______ to do and so [3.] ______ people stay at home. If they have saved [4.] ______ money, young people book cheap flights to Majorca and spend [5.] ______ days there. It's just about a thousand miles away. After [6.] ______ hours they land in Majorca, where [7.] ______ of them enjoy parties and have [8.] ______ fun.

5 Prepositions

► Some important prepositions, p. 177

Fill in suitable prepositions from the box.

at – at – at – at – at – on – on – on – in – in – in – in – in – by – by – past – until – to – to

Arriving in London

When Melinda landed [1.] at London Gatwick Airport [2.] ______ a Saturday [3.] ______ June she arrived just [4.] ______ time for the Wimbledon tennis championships. She is very interested [5.] ______ sports and so she tried to get some tickets. First she went to the city centre [6.] ______ train and then she went [7.] ______ a ticket office [8.] ______ foot. When she arrived [9.] ______ five minutes [10.] ______ six, she found that the office had just closed [11.] ______ six o'clock. So she went to her hostel [12.] ______ bus. [13.] ______ the hostel she booked tickets [14.] ______ the Internet there. Later on [15.] ______ the evening she went [16.] ______ the cinema and watched the latest Leonardo di Caprio film. She came back to her hostel [17.] ______ midnight and slept [18.] ______ 9 o'clock [19.] ______ the morning.

6 Adjectives

a) Write the forms of comparison of the adjectives in the box under the suitable heading. ► Comparison of adjectives, p. 178

small – beautiful – good – easy – big – cheap – difficult – nice – heavy – tall – attractive – elegant – hungry – bad – much – intelligent – happy – hot – little – large – interesting – healthy

Adjective	-er	-est
small	smaller	smallest
easy	easier	easiest

Adjective	more	most
beautiful	more beautiful	most beautiful

Adjective	irregular (unregelmäßig)	irregular (unregelmäßig)
good	better	best

b) **Study the following example and compare the phones and the buildings below.**

Example:
1. **Mobile phone 2 is cheaper than mobile phone 3.**
2. **Mobile phone 2 is not as cheap as phone 1.**
3. **Mobile phone 1 is the cheapest.**

Empire State Building (381 m), USA

Shanghai Tower (632 m), China

Burj Khalifa (828 m), Dubai

1. Mobile phone 3 is more expensive than ______________________
2. Mobile phone 1 is ______________________
3. Mobile phone 3 is ______________________

____

____

____

____

____

____

7 Question tags

a) **Complete the sentences with suitable question tags from the box.** ► Question tags, p. 188

aren't you – isn't she – don't you – don't they – haven't they – won't they – won't you – is she – have they – aren't they

Meeting a person and asking questions in a polite way

1. You are from Boston, aren't you ?
2. You live in Liverpool, don't you ?
3. Your friend Tracy isn't from Boston, is she ?
4. Tracy is from England, ______________ ?
5. Tracy and Sharon are staying in Paris at the moment, ______________ ?
6. They love France, ______________ ?
7. They have been to France several times, ______________ ?
8. But they haven't seen the Port of Marseille yet, ______________ ?
9. They will come back next week, ______________ ?
10. You will meet them at the airport, ______________ ?

b) **Complete the following sentences with suitable question tags on your own.**

The development of our planet

1. Many people are worried about our nature, ____________________?
2. They do not believe in a positive development, ____________________?
3. The earth is getting warmer, ____________________?
4. We are consuming too much water, ____________________?
5. We haven't paid enough attention to our environment, ____________________?
6. Last year, people bought more cars than in the years before, ____________________?
7. We can all do something, ____________________?
8. You will come to our meeting tomorrow, ____________________?

8 Possessive case – Whose?

► Possessive case, p. 177

Fill in the missing word.

1. This book belongs to Jerry. It is Jerry's book.
2. Only girls go to this school. It is a girls' school.
3. This laptop belongs to my parents. It is my ____________ laptop.
4. The Smiths own this house. This is the ____________ house.
5. The children are playing with their toys. These are the ____________ toys.
6. This secretary works for the Prime Minister. She is the ____________ secretary.
7. Those people have to look after patients at a hospital. Caring for patients is those ____________ duty.
8. I bought this newspaper yesterday. It is ____________ newspaper.

9 Word order

► Word order with adverbs and adverbials, p. 180

Put the following parts of the sentences in the right order.

Christmas shopping

1. a lot of people and cars / in the streets / there are
   There are a lot of people and cars in the streets.
2. quickly / walking / to the bus stop / are / some people
   ____
3. at the red lights / the cars / waiting / at the moment / are
   ____
4. crossing / some shoppers / the street / in a hurry / are
   ____
5. lots of presents / they / bought / in the department stores / have / already
   ____
6. to their children / these presents / on Christmas Day / they / want to give
   ____

Unit 1

Young people in the world of work

A | Getting started: First steps into the world of work

1 Young people's posts ► Vokabeln systematisch lernen, S. 238

Find the words and phrases in the texts which match the following definitions.

Post Emma (→ page 8)

1.	training for a few weeks or months (often not paid) in order to get work experience	
2.	understanding of a new situation or a new job	
3.	in a foreign country	
4.	make arrangements at hotel reception when you arrive and want to stay there	

Post Tom (→ page 9)

5.	school for young children	
6.	parts of a city that are furthest away from the centre	
7.	trip to a place of interest	

Post Zuzanna (→ page 18)

8.	a building or room in which you can do experiments	
9.	things you need for a hobby or work	
10.	something you do in a regular way	

B | Grammar

2 Introducing a person ► Present simple, p. 183

Complete the following text about Tracy using the verbs in the box.

be – have (2×) – love – play – drive – come – live – work – chat

Hi! I would like to introduce my friend Tracy. She [1.] ____________ seventeen years old and she [2.] ____________ from England. She [3.] ____________ a brother and a sister. They [4.] ____________ in a flat in Liverpool. Tracy's mother [5.] ____________ as a nurse and her father [6.] ____________ a bus. Tracy [7.] ____________ a part-time job in a fast food restaurant. In her free time she [8.] ____________ with friends on the Internet or [9.] ____________ volleyball. She [10.] ____________ her cats 'Trisha' and 'Trix'.

3 At college

► Present simple, p. 183

Ask and answer questions using the prompts given.

1. enjoy languages? (yes) Do you enjoy languages? – Yes, I do.
2. like maths? (no) Do you like maths? – No, I don't.
3. be interested in sports? (yes) Are you interested in sports? – Yes, I am.
4. eat lunch at college? (yes) ______
5. prefer IT to English? (no) ______
6. start college at half past nine? (no) ______
7. go home by bus? (yes) ______
8. take tests in every subject? (yes) ______
9. have exams? (yes) ______
10. be nervous before exams? (yes) ______

4 What are they doing?

► Present continuous, p. 184

Say what the following persons are doing and what they are not doing.

1. **Example: Will – cycle?** Is Will cycling? – No, Will is not cycling, he is driving a car.
2. **Example: Sue and Ellen – send text messages?** Are Sue and Ellen sending text messages? – No, they are not sending text messages, they are talking on the phone.
3. Marco – sleep? ______
4. Lisa and Sam – talk? ______
5. Sarah – work? ______

6. Sabrina – watch TV? ______

______

7. Julio – sing? ______

______

8. The girls – play volleyball? ______

5 After college

► Present simple, p. 183 ► Present continuous, p. 184

a) **Complete the following list of tense markers with the words from the box.**

now – normally – this afternoon – today – every weekend – at the moment – right now – every Monday – on Sundays – usually – regularly

Tense markers

Present simple	Present continuous
normally	now

b) **Complete the following text. Watch out for the correct tenses.**

After college Lucy and Stan normally **[1. work]** work part-time at Macy's Superstore but they **[2. not work]** are not working there now. Stan is sick and **[3. stay]** ______ home this afternoon. Usually Stan **[4. go]** ______ to the store by bike but right now his sister Anna **[5. use]** ______ it because she has to do the shopping today. **[6. want]** ______ she ______ to go shopping? No, Anna **[7. not like]** ______ shopping. Anna's friend Lucy **[8. take]** ______ part in a sports competition with another college today. Every Monday she **[9. train]** ______ at college with some other girls from her course and they regularly **[10. meet]** ______ at a friend's house and **[11. practise]** ______ for more than three hours. At the moment Lucy and her friends **[12. stand]** ______ in front of the gym and **[13. wait]** ______ for the beginning of the competition.

6 Managing situations

M

► Present simple, p. 183 ► Present continuous, p. 184

a) **Sagen Sie einem englischsprachigen Gast, …**

1. dass Sie das Kolleg besuchen. ______
2. welche Fächer Sie mögen bzw. nicht mögen. ______
3. ob Sie am Nachmittag / Abend / Wochenende arbeiten. ______
4. was Sie zurzeit tun. ______

b) **Fragen Sie Ihren Gast, ...**

1. woher er / sie kommt. ______
2. wie lange er / sie bleibt. ______
3. wie ihm / ihr Ihr Ort gefällt. ______
4. ob er / sie Deutsch spricht. ______

C | Reading: Living and working in London

7 Let's share the flat! – Verbs and nouns → page 12

Complete the following list of words from the text with suitable verbs or nouns.

	Verb	Noun
1.	to decide	
2.	to communicate	
3.		placement
4.		checkout
5.	to improve	
6.	to share	
7.		life
8.		trouble
9.	to guess	
10.	to sound	

8 Let's share the flat! – Antonyms → page 12

Find the opposites (antonyms) of the following words and phrases in the text.

1.	decreasing	
2.	to stay in one's home country	
3.	to keep all of it for oneself	
4.	worse	
5.	boring	
6.	packing	

7.	unfortunately	
8.	badly	
9.	the same	
10.	from one's own country	
11.	to make worse	
12.	together	

D | Practice

9 Training skills – How to describe pictures

► Fotos und Illustrationen beschreiben / analysieren, S. 211

a) **Complete the following description of the photo by filling in verbs from the box below and the phrases given in the picture.**

concentrate – hold – lean – prepare – seem – **show** – stand – train – try – use – want – wear

The colour photo [1.] shows a scene in a restaurant kitchen. Three people [2.] ________ in front of a stove in the [3.] ________. On the [4.] ________ we can see a young woman who [5.] ________ a pan. In the [6.] ________ a young man [7.] ________ a ladle to show soup to an older man on the [8.] ________ who [9.] ________ forward in order to have a better look. The two younger people [10.] ________ white working clothes while the older person has a dark shirt on. He [11.] ________ to be the head chef. Perhaps he [12.] ________ to taste the soup. In the [13.] ________ on the left we can see another young person who [14.] ________ meals. All the people are busy and [15.] ________ on their work. Maybe all these young people [16.] ________ to become chefs and [17.] ________ to do their very best.

P b) **Describe and analyze the following photo in a similar way. The words in the box may help you.**

to hike – countryside – backpack – hiking stick – map – walking-tour – hiker

10 Jobs

Fill in the following crossword puzzle with suitable English words from pages 14 and 15 in your student's book.

ACROSS

4. Freizeit
7. Ratschlag
8. Wohnung
9. Verkäufer(in)
10. Vordergrund
12. Miete
13. ermüdend
14. teilen

DOWN

1. Lohn
2. Koch
3. draußen
5. Hintergrund
6. Praktikum
11. nicht mögen

E | Reading +

11 Work on a farm – and see the world for free → page 16

Complete the summary using suitable words from the text "Work on a farm . . .".

If you are interested in travelling the world but you cannot afford it, a "Work and **[1.]** Travel programme may be for you. There are many projects in Australia and New Zealand which offer free **[2.]** ____________ and **[3.]** ____________ to people who are prepared to work on **[4.]** ____________. The **[5.]** ____________ of your stay is flexible. You can stay for a few weeks or for **[6.]** ____________ months. This must be **[7.]** ____________ with the farm owners. You can learn or do many different things but before accepting an offer **[8.]** ____________ carefully what is **[9.]** ____________ of you. Eight hours of **[10.]** ____________ labour can be hard for an untrained person. If you are not sure about your **[11.]** ____________ so far from home, you should travel with a friend. Before deciding look on the Internet for **[12.]** ____________ from former travellers. The WWOOF groups offer a **[13.]** ____________ of hosts. First you have to join one of the groups which can cost you up to **[14.]** ____________.

Unit 2
Getting a job

A | Getting started: Big companies

1 A name behind many names → page 21 ► Vokabeln systematisch lernen, S. 238

Find synonyms for the following words in the text. Fill in the suitable form of the word and the line where you have found it.

	Word	Synonym in the text	Line
1.	to establish		
2.	to put a product on the market		
3.	highly		
4.	famous		
5.	to rise		
6.	goods		
7.	in the meantime		
8.	to buy		
9.	to concentrate		

2 International markets ► Vokabeln systematisch lernen, S. 238

Complete the following list of geographical regions with countries from the box below (four countries per region).

Korea – Chile – Lebanon – Namibia – Bolivia – Cameroon – Japan – Nigeria – Iran – Iraq – Argentina – Saudi Arabia – Brazil – Vietnam – Indonesia – Angola

1.	Latin America	
2.	Africa	
3.	the Middle East	
4.	Asia	

B | Grammar

3 The development of a company

► Past simple, p. 185

a) **Complete the following text about *The Times* by using the right forms of the verbs in the simple past.**

John Walter ___was___ the first editor of *The Times* newspaper in 1785. He ___called___ it *The Daily Universal Register* at that time but it ___did not become___ popular under this name. So Walter **[1. change]** __________ the title to *The Times* three years later. In 1803 he **[2. hand]** __________ the newspaper over to his son. At that time the profits of *The Times* **[3. be]** __________ high because there **[4. not be]** __________ many other newspapers on the market. Walter **[5. have]** __________ very good writers because he **[6. pay]** __________ them very well. The influence of *The Times* **[7. rise]** __________ even more by the beginning of the 19th century. The newspaper was the first that **[8. send]** __________ war correspondents to write about conflicts in other countries. Different people **[9. own]** __________ *The Times* in the following years. It **[10. not be]** __________ until 1966 that *The Times* **[11. print]** __________ news on its front page, previously it only **[12. publish]** __________ small advertisements there. In 1981 the Australian Rupert Murdoch **[13. buy]** __________ *The Times* and **[14. introduce]** __________ new computer technology.

b) **Make questions about the following words taken from the text above.**

1. *The Daily Universal Register* ___What did John Walter call the newspaper first?___
2. three years later
____
3. because there were not many other newspapers on the market
____
4. very well
____
5. war correspondents
____
6. news
____
7. new computer technology
____

4 Preparing for an interview

► Past simple, p. 185 ► Present perfect simple, p. 186

a) **Greg Wilson has a job interview tomorrow. He has made some notes in order to prepare for the interview. Underline the time expressions in the notes and decide which tense you must use with these time expressions.**

b) **Make complete sentences about Greg in the correct tense.**

Examples:

1. born in 1992 (simple past) Greg was born in 1992.
2. school until 2008 (simple past) He went to school until 2008.
3. interested in computers for a long time now (present perfect simple)
He has been interested in computers for a long time now.
4. live / in Liverpool / from 1992 to 1996 (______)
5. family / move / to Birmingham / in 1996 (______)
6. live / in Birmingham / since then (______)
7. join / a computer club / four years ago (______)
8. pass / exams / in 2008 (______)
9. find / a good job training programme / after his exams (______)
10. be / with that company / for a few years now (______)

5 For or since?

► Present perfect simple, p. 186 ► Present perfect continuous, p. 187

Re-write the following sentences by replacing "since" or "for" and by changing the time expression.

Example: It's Monday now. Simon hasn't seen Jane since Friday.

Simon hasn't seen Jane for three days.

1. It's October 15 now. Sally has been ill for two weeks.
Sally has been ill since ...
2. It's the end of August now. It hasn't rained in Cornwall for a month now.
3. It's Friday evening now. The manager has been in China since Monday morning.
4. It's Christmas now. Sarah hasn't had a big party since last Christmas.
5. It's half past ten now. Nick has been watching TV for four hours now.

6 A job interview ► Past simple, p. 185 ► Present perfect simple, p. 186

Complete the following job interview between Judy Hill and Susan Sunday by filling in the right forms of the verbs in the past simple or present perfect simple.

Judy: Hello there, Susan. First of all, can you tell me something about yourself?

Susan: I **[1. be born]** ______________ in York on September 2nd 1994. I **[2. live]** ______________ there for four years. Then we all **[3. move]** ______________ to Swindon because my father **[4. find]** ______________ a better job there.

Judy: **[5. go]** ______________ you ______________ to school in Swindon then?

Susan: Yes, I **[6. do]** ______________ ! I **[7. attend]** ______________ school there until 2010.

Judy: I see from your application that you **[8. be]** ______________ interested in designing clothes for a long time. At what age **[9. start]** ______________ you ______________ that?

Susan: It all **[10. begin]** ______________ when I **[11. spend]** ______________ a holiday with my aunt about six or seven years ago. She not only **[12. teach]** ______________ me to design clothes but also how to make my own dresses. So in the last few years I **[13. make]** ______________ quite a lot of clothes – not only for myself but also for friends.

Judy: **[14. do]** ______________ you already ______________ a placement in that field?

Susan: I **[15. not do]** ______________ a placement yet but I **[16. take]** ______________ some courses at college in the past few months. And in my last summer holidays I **[17. help]** ______________ my aunt in her clothes shop. I **[18. enjoy]** ______________ that very much. That's one reason why I **[19. apply]** ______________ to your company.

7 Managing situations ► Past simple, p. 185 ► Present perfect simple, p. 186

M

Sie haben sich bei einem internationalen Unternehmen um einen Ausbildungsplatz beworben. Ein Teil Ihres Bewerbungsgesprächs findet deshalb auf Englisch statt. Sagen Sie dem Interviewer / der Interviewerin, dass Sie . . .

1. schon viel über das Unternehmen gehört haben.

____

2. sich im Internet über das Unternehmen informiert haben.

____

3. erst vor einem Jahr hierher gezogen sind.

____

4. bereits ein Praktikum absolviert haben.

____

5. schon immer für ein internationales Unternehmen arbeiten wollten.

____

C | Reading

8 Applications → pages 24 / 25

Match the phrases on the left with suitable phrases on the right to make meaningful sentences according to the documents in your student's book.

1.		Julia is a student	a)	basic computer skills in Word and Excel.
2.		She would like to apply	b)	to going to the interview at the hotel.
3.		Julia is interested	c)	of French and Spanish.
4.		She has experience	d)	for a job placement in London.
5.		The young woman has a good working knowledge	e)	for a person who is able to work in a team.
6.		The hotel is looking	f)	in working at a hotel.
7.		The hotel needs a person who has	g)	in working part-time at a hotel.
8.		The applicant is looking forward	h)	at a college of further education.

D | Practice

9 Finding the right candidate → page 26 ► Vokabeln systematisch lernen, S. 238

Fill in the complete names of the jobs mentioned in task D1 by matching the parts on the left with parts on the right.

1.	personnel m ...	a)	technician
2.	motor	b)	manager
3.	computer	c)	person
4.	laboratory	d)	therapist
5.	bank	e)	mechanic
6.	nursery school	f)	clerk
7.	sales	g)	assistant
8.	physio	h)	teacher

10 A placement on offer

Complete the following text about two students by filling in "ed" or "ing".

1. Julia is interest______ in finding a work placement in Britain.
2. She is really motivat______ and has already written several applications.
3. She hopes that a placement abroad could be very interest______.
4. When she receives some answers from British companies she gets excit______.
5. Of course, positive reactions to her applications are motivat______.
6. One offer seems excit______. Julia could do a placement in a holiday resort on the Isle of Wight!

E | Reading +

11 Training skills – How to describe statistics

► Diagramme beschreiben / analysieren, S. 215

a) Match the names of the graphs in the box with the pictures.

pie chart – line graph – bar chart

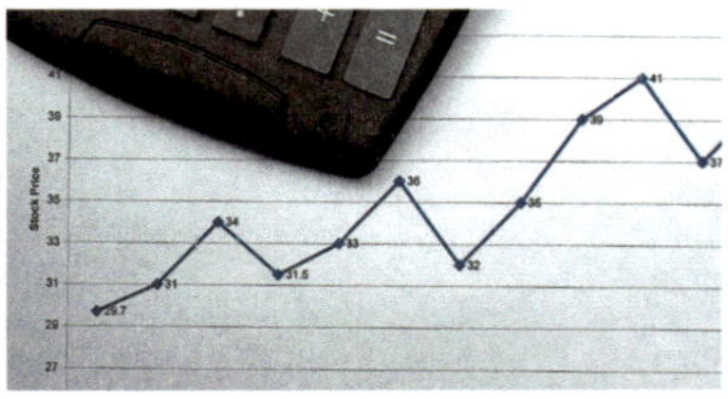

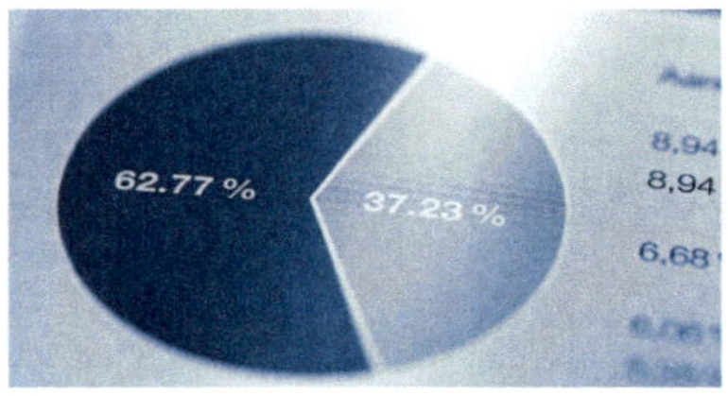

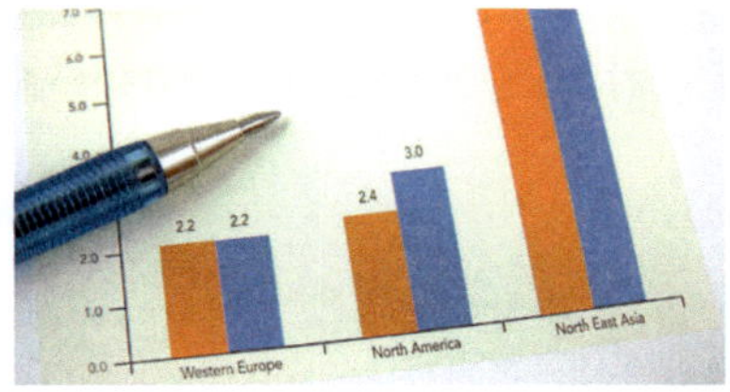

1. ______________________ 2. ______________________ 3. ______________________

b) Read the description of the following pie chart, complete the last sentence and fill in the data in the chart.

This pie chart shows the different age groups at YOUR HOST INTERNATIONAL. 10 per cent of the staff are younger than 20. The percentage of those between 30 and 39 amounts to 25 per cent. 18 per cent of YHO's staff are between 40 and 49. The most important group is the 20-to-29-year olds at about 40 per cent.

Only [1.] ______________ per cent of the employees are [2.] ______________ years or older.

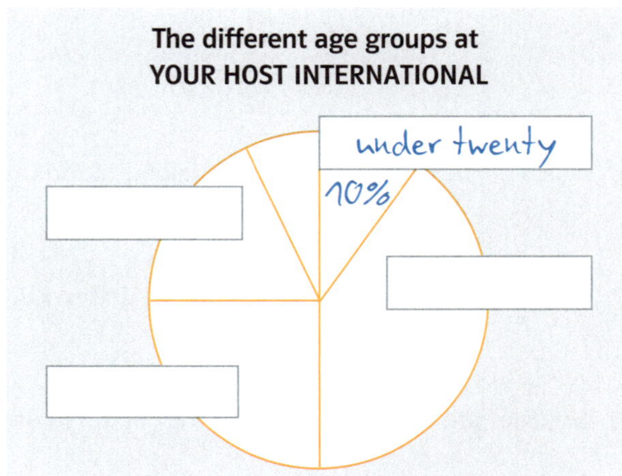

c) Complete the description of the bar chart below.

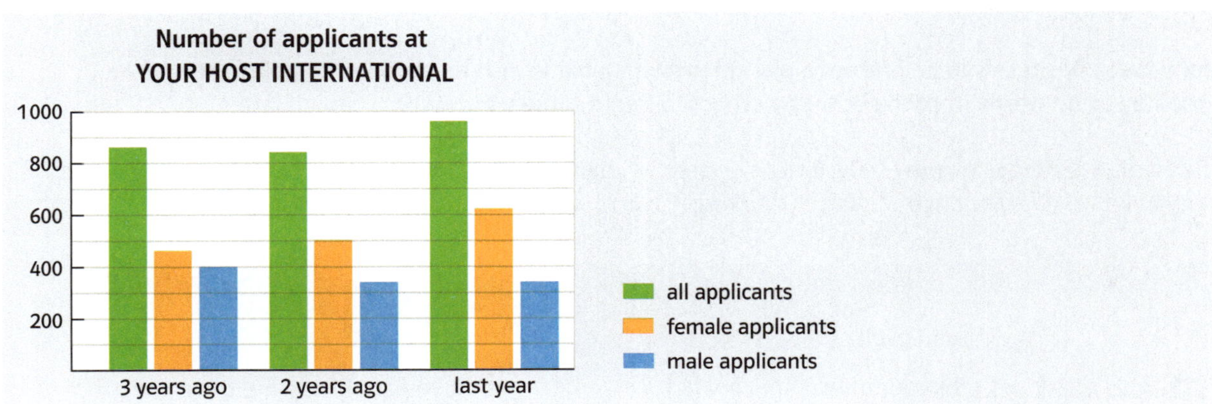

This [1.] ______________ chart shows the development of the number of [2.] ______________ for a job at YOUR HOST INTERNATIONAL: Three years ago the number totalled 860 with [3.] ______________ women and 400 men. In the following year the number of applicants [4.] ______________ slightly to 840 although the number of women significantly [5.] ______________ by 40. So the number of male applicants fell sharply by [6.] ______________ per cent. Last year the total number grew [7.] ______________ to 960. The number of male applicants [8.] ______________ at the same level while the number of female applicants [9.] ______________ again.

Unit A

Preparing for a work placement in London

1 England, Britain or the UK?

a) Fill in the names of the countries and their capitals as shown on the map.

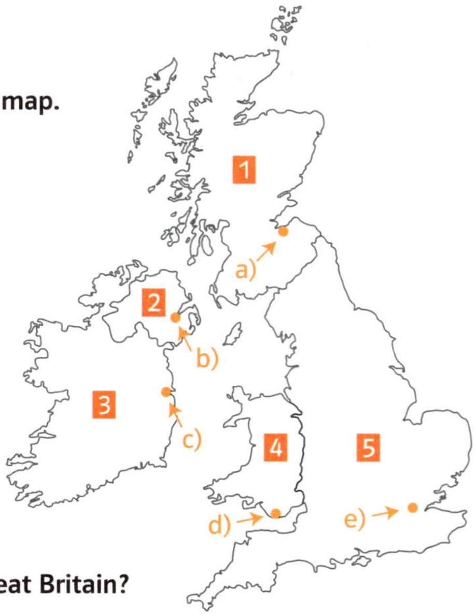

1.		a)	
2.		b)	
3.		c)	
4.		d)	
5.		e)	

b) Which of the countries does not belong to the United Kingdom?

____

c) Which of the countries belongs to the United Kingdom but not to Great Britain?

____

d) Which of the capitals is not only the capital of one country but also the capital of the United Kingdom?

____

2 Writing an e-mail

Jenny Lucas has received an offer of a placement with a big British newspaper. Complete her e-mail by using words from the box. Remember to begin some words with a capital letter.

forward – getting to know – placement – dear – thank you very much – yours sincerely – as you know – experience – glad – working

[1.] __________ Mr Lovell

[2.] __________ for your offer. I am very [3.] __________ that you are giving me the chance of [4.] __________ the production of a big newspaper from the inside. [5.] __________ I am doing a [6.] __________ at our local newspaper but working at your company will be a great [7.] __________ for me. I look [8.] __________ to [9.] __________ with you.

[10.] __________

Jenny Lucas

3 Making a phone call

a) Choose suitable words from the box and fill them in.

check – sorry – reduction – lot – vacancies – help – is – offer – far – spell – moment

1. Can I ________________ you?
2. Do you have any ________________ ?
3. Just a ________________ , please.
4. Let me ________________ this for you.
5. How much ________________ the room, please?
6. How ________________ is your hotel from the station?
7. I'm ________________ . We don't ________________ lunch.
8. I can give you a ________________ of 10 per cent.
9. Could you ________________ your name for me, please?
10. Thanks a ________________ .

b) Put the following parts of a telephone conversation in the right order. Write the corresponding numbers before the sentences.

		Receptionist
	A	Let me just check. – That would be alright for two weeks.
1	B	Hello. This is Edinburgh 3029483. Clare Duncan speaking. How can I help you?
	C	Thank you very much, Ms Lucas. We look forward to welcoming you on the tenth then.
	D	Do you need a single room or a double room?
	E	That will be £40.
	F	And when exactly would you arrive, Ms Lucas?
	H	I'm sorry. Breakfast is £10 extra.
	H	Would you just give me your name again, please, and your credit card details?

		Caller
	I	A single room, please.
	J	That's OK. Is breakfast included in the price?
	K	Fine. How much is the room, please?
2	L	Hello. My name's Jenny Lucas. I'm looking for a room for two weeks.
	M	On the tenth of next month. Do you have any vacancies then?
	N	So that's £50 per night then. I'll take it. How can I make a booking?
	O	Well, my name is Jenny Lucas – J-e-n-n-y-L-u-c-a-s. And I've got a SmartCard No. 2432 5436 7654 6789.
	P	Thank you for your help, bye-bye.

Unit 3
The youth market

A | Getting started: Young people as consumers

1 Young consumers hold the key to change
► Vokabeln systematisch lernen, S. 238

Match the following words and phrases with suitable definitions by filling in the right letter.

1.		to give a product an environmentally-friendly image	a)	brand
2.		a group of products that are all made by one company and all have the same name	b)	principle
3.		a rule or belief which helps you to decide what is right or wrong	c)	figures
4.		to make less confident or less hopeful	d)	to confuse
5.		to make someone uncertain or unable to understand something; to make something difficult to understand	e)	to greenwash
6.		to give a product the image of being produced in humane working conditions	f)	to discourage
7.		numbers which show an amount (e.g. of money)	g)	label
8.		the name of a clothing manufacturer or fashion designer	h)	to fairwash

B | Grammar

2 Shop till your drop
► Past simple, p. 185 ► Past perfect simple, p. 187

Describe Julia's shopping trip in complete sentences as in the examples.

Example 1:
10:20 leaves home / 10:30 takes the bus to the shopping centre

After Julia had left home she took the bus to the shopping centre.

Example 2:
10:50 drinks a cup of coffee / 10:45 (!) arrives at the shopping centre

Julia drank a cup of coffee after she had arrived at the shopping centre.

1. 11:00 enters the chemist's / 11:10 buys a bottle of shampoo

2. 11:30 tries on some trainers / 11:20 looks at new fitness equipment

3. 11:50 meets her friend Jenny / 12:00 have lunch together

4. 12:30 Jenny leaves / 12:45 Julia continues with her shopping

5. 13:15 goes to a clothes shop / 13:00 buys a magazine

6. 14:15 tries on some new clothes for an hour / 14:20 decides to go to the supermarket

7. 14:40 goes to the cash desk / 14:30 puts milk, bread and meat into her shopping basket

8. 14:50 leaves the shopping centre / 15:00 takes the bus home

3 A car crash on the way home

► Past simple, p. 185 ► Past continuous, p. 185

When Julia was coming home from the shops a few days ago, she saw a car crash and called the police. Afterwards she had to answer the following questions.

Example 1:

Police officer: Julia, what were you doing when you saw the crash? **[cross the street]**

Julia: I was crossing the street.

Example 2:

Police officer: Julia, what did you do then? **[call the ambulance and the police]**

Julia: I called the ambulance and the police.

1. Police officer: Where was the car coming from? **[petrol station]**

   Julia:

2. Police officer: What was the driver doing? **[use / mobile phone]**

   Julia:

3. Police officer: What did his car hit the school bus? [not watch / the traffic]
   Julia: ______________________________

4. Police officer: What was the school bus driver doing? [talk / to a pupil on the bus]
   Julia: ______________________________

5. Police officer: What happened to the two vehicles? [crash / in the middle of the street]
   Julia: ______________________________

6. Police officer: What did you do after you had phoned us? [get on / the school bus]
   Julia: ______________________________

7. Police officer: What were the pupils doing when you entered the bus? [cry]
   Julia: ______________________________

4 Home at last ► Past simple, p. 185 ► Past continuous, p. 185

Use "while" or "when" to describe what happened or what was happening when Julia finally got home.

1. unpack / her bags – telephone / ring
   While/when Julia was unpacking her bags the telephone rang.
2. count / her money – drop / some coins
   ____
3. put / the food in the fridge – neighbour / knock / on the door
   ____
4. talk / to the neighbour – cat / run out
   ____
5. look for / cat – another accident / happen

Now go on. Make two more sentences in the same way.

____

____

5 The successful introduction of a new product ► pages 183 – 187

Fill in the suitable tense to complete the following text.

When the 2W advertising agency [1. get] got the chance to develop the advertising campaign for the new "CrispChoc" six months ago they [2. be] were very happy because it [3. be] had been hard work to persuade the biscuits producers. While they [4. work] __________ on the project they [5. have] __________ to work long hours, even at the weekends. But after they [6. find] __________ the suitable key words 2W [7. invent] __________ a slogan which [8. become] __________ really successful in the past few months. In the meantime the biscuit company [9. sell] __________ millions of boxes of "CrispChoc". Of course, 2W [10. work] __________ on a new project now.

C | Reading

6 Buyers' training at schools → page 40

a) **Find suitable synonyms or antonyms in the text and fill them in the following tables.**

	Find a synonym for this word or phrase	Word or phrase in the text
1.	a few	
2.	require	
3.	to start, to launch	
4.	very important	
5.	80 %	
6.	up-to-date	
7.	to try hard	
8.	convinced	
9.	use money to pay	
10.	reasonable, wise to do	

	Find an antonym for this word or phrase	Word or phrase in the text
1.	difficult	
2.	oldest, out of fashion	
3.	high	
4.	off-line	
5.	more	
6.	to spend	
7.	minor	
8.	to reject, to refuse	
9.	most expensive	
10.	carelessly	

b) **Complete the following text with suitable words from the tables above.**

Many young people are [1.] ________________ in debt because they [2.] ________________ more money than they really have. For example they buy the [3.] ________________ mobile phone because they are [4.] ________________ that this is cool and will show that they are [5.] ________________.
Now, schools have [6.] ________________ a new programme which will help young people to manage their money. There young people learn that it is [7.] ________________ to plan future expenses and first to [8.] ________________ money so that they can then afford [9.] ________________ purchases. So next time you go [10.] ________________ ask yourself if you really [11.] ________________ the product or service and if you have the money before you click the "Buy" button.

7 Managing situations – Helping customers ► pages 183 – 187

M

Sie bedienen einen englischsprachigen Kunden in einem Fotofachgeschäft. Sie fragen den Kunden, ...

1. wie Sie ihm helfen können.
2. wo er die Anzeige für die Digitalkamera gesehen hat.
3. ob er die Digitalkamera schon ausprobiert hat.
4. wie er sich gefühlt hat, als er die Digitalkamera ausprobiert hat.
5. ob er seine alte Digitalkamera noch mochte, nachdem er die neue ausprobiert hatte.

Bitte schreiben Sie die Fragen in Ihr Heft.

1. How can I help you?

8 Training skills – How to do a role play → page 41

a) **Put the following parts of a sales talk in the right order.**

	Sales assistant
	This netbook has a 10 inch screen and Internet access and it's not too expensive.
	No problem, sir. This here is our latest netbook. Would you be interested in learning some more about it?
1	Good morning, sir, how can I help you?
	We have a special offer today. It's only $199.
	Of course, sir. We have a wide range of laptops. What are you especially interested in?
	Thank you very much.
	No problem. The white one is the same price.
	You're welcome.

	Customer
	That would be nice.
	Well, I'd like to have a small one which I can put in my briefcase.
	How much is this model?
	That's fine. I'll take it.
2	Good morning. I'm interested in laptops. Have you got any special offers?
	And what about different colours? I'd prefer a white one.
	Thank you for your help.

b) **Find phrases in the sales talk above (8 a) which have a similar meaning to the following.**

1. How much does this laptop cost? How much is this model?
2. Would you like to have some more information about it? ____
3. That would be fine. ____
4. Do you offer different colours? ____
5. Thanks a lot for your assistance. ____
6. I'd like to have it. ____
7. I'd like a white laptop better. ____
8. Certainly, sir. ____
9. What can I do for you? ____
10. It only costs … ____
11. My pleasure. ____
12. No worries, sir. ____

c) **Now play or re-write the dialogue (8 a). Change as many phrases as possible.**

D | Practice

9 Advertising

Complete the crossword on the right and find the solution by filling in the corresponding English words for the German key words.

1. Kampagne, Werbefeldzug
2. Verlangen, Wunsch
3. Kurzform für Werbeanzeige
4. Zielgruppe (zwei Wörter)
5. (Verkaufs-)Förderung
6. Aufmerksamkeit
7. Preis
8. Interesse
9. Medien
10. umgehen mit
11. Firmen- oder Markenzeichen, Logo

12. einführen, auf den Markt bringen
13. Werbemelodie
14. Werbesendung, Spot
15. Werbespruch, Werbeslogan
16. Handeln, Aktion
17. Unternehmen

							Solution ▼								
1.															
2.															
3.															
4.															
5.															
6.															
7.															
8.															
9.															
10.															
11.															
12.															
13.															
14.															
15.															
16.															
17.															

E | Reading +: New trends in advertising

10 Digital advertising on the move

Fill in the missing words of the following word families.

	Verb	Noun	Adjective
1.	to interest		
2.		effect	
3.			informative
4.	to differ		
5.		reliance, reliability	
6.			special
7.	to regulate		
8.		creator, creation	
9.			live, alive
10.	to succeed		
11.		use, user	
12.			integrative

Unit 4

Media in our lives

A | Getting started

1 Watching TV → page 49 ► Vokabeln systematisch lernen, S. 238

With the help of the syllables in the box below write down ten words which appear in the text. The first syllable of each word has already been given. Each line represents a syllable.

a – ca – cade – cant – di – ence – ence – er – er – fer – fi – it – ment – mu – ni – ni – tain – ter – ti – tion – tions – tude

1. view ___
2. de ___
3. sig ___ ___ ___
4. at ___ ___
5. dif ___ ___
6. au ___ ___
7. gen ___ ___ ___
8. en ___ ___ ___
9. hab ___
10. com ___ ___ ___ ___

B | Grammar

2 Can you help me? – At the internet café ► Will-future, p. 188

Write the staff member's polite offers in complete sentences.

Example:
Customer: **I'd like to have a coffee, please.**
Staff member: **[serve / in a minute]** I'll serve it in a minute.

1. Customer: I don't know how to access the Internet.
   Staff: **[help / you]** ______________________
   ____
2. Customer: There is no mouse here.
   Staff: **[bring / you / one]** ______________________
3. Customer: What's the Internet address of the nearest hostel, please?
   Staff: **[look it up / for you]** ______________________
4. Customer: How can I print this out?
   Staff: **[do it / for you]** ______________________
5. Customer: I'd like to make an Internet phone call, please.
   Staff: **[show / you]** ______________________
6. Customer: I'd like to pay, please.
   Staff: **[be with you / in a minute]** ______________________

3 What will your life and world be like in 50 years' time? ► Will-future, p. 188

What do you suppose your life will be like in 50 years' time?
Make meaningful sentences using "probably, suppose, expect, think, I'm afraid, I'm sure".

Example: sit / in front of a monitor / all day
I (do not) think that I / we / people will sit in front of a monitor all day.

1. be / commercials on TV / most of the time ______
2. people / not talk / to each other any more ______
3. use / mobile phones ______
4. go / by car ______
5. live / on Mars ______
6. life / be / more comfortable than today ______

4 What are they going to do next? – Media at work ► Future with 'going to', p. 187

a) **Match the first step in the box below with a suitable second step.**

	▼	First step
1.	c	**The assistant has just written an e-mail.**
2.		The trainee has just opened his / her laptop.
3.		The manager has just looked up a telephone number.
4.		The secretary is just opening the word processing program.
5.		The employee has just bought a sandwich at the cafeteria.
6.		The technical assistant has installed a new program.
7.		The secretary has just written a letter.

	Second step
a)	write a letter
b)	make a call
c)	**send it**
d)	turn it on
e)	test it
f)	put it in an envelope
g)	eat it

b) **Write down what the people in 4 a) are going to do in complete sentences. Use a separate sheet of paper.**

Example: 1. c) The assistant is going to send it.

5 Which media should we use? – A discussion at an advertising agency

► Will-future, p. 188 ► Future with 'going to', p. 187

Fill in the suitable form of 'going to' or 'will' in order to complete the following conversation.

Henry: According to our plans we are going to start the new advertising campaign in time for the winter season. I think it will be best to advertise in local newspapers.

Annie: It is a quality product so I expect that sales [1.] __________ be better if we advertise in quality magazines.

George: How about radio commercials? Perhaps we [2.] __________ reach more customers in this way.

Trisha: Don't forget the Internet. It's a product for young people, too. It [3.] __________ probably be the best way to address them.

Henry: That's a good idea! I [4.] __________ phone InterAD right after our meeting and arrange that.

Annie: Don't forget that George has an appointment with the team from RadioTeen. He [5.] __________ to talk to them about new conditions. Perhaps a mix of radio and Internet advertising [6.] __________ be best.

6 Managing situations – Talking about the future

M

► Will-future, p. 188 ► Future with 'going to', p. 187

Sie chatten mit einem / r englischsprachigen Freund(in) und schreiben, dass ...

1. Sie wahrscheinlich Ihre Prüfung bestehen werden.
2. Sie annehmen, dass es genügend Zeit zum Lernen geben wird.
3. Sie ihn / sie bestimmt in Ihren nächsten Ferien besuchen werden.
4. Sie sich ein neues Computerprogramm gekauft haben und es heute Abend ausprobieren werden.
5. Ihre Mutter Sie gerade gebeten hat, ihr zu helfen, und Sie in zehn Minuten wieder zurück sein werden.

1.
2.
3.
4.
5.

C | Reading

7 You can't escape it! → page 52 ► Mit Texten ohne Wörterbuch umgehen, S. 232

Match words from list A with suitable words from list B – according to the texts.

	▼	A
1.		to place
2.		to download
3.		to post
4.		to target
5.		to offer
6.		to pay
7.		to send
8.		to warn
9.		to approach
10.		to use
11.		to commit
12.		to do

	B		
a)	ideas	g)	music
b)	children	h)	deposits
c)	students	i)	investigations
d)	false identities	j)	rooms
e)	Internet users	k)	e-mails
f)	bets	l)	a crime

D | Practice

8 What's on the radio? → page 54 ► Vokabeln systematisch lernen, S. 238

Complete the phrases in the list below with one of the words in the box.

of – of – on – out – out – to – to – to – to – with

1.	according	
2.	to check	
3.	in order	
4.	to be aware	
5.	the use	
6.	to find	
7.	to have access	
8.	to be obsessed	
9.	to be addicted	
10.	to have an effect	

9 Training skills – How to describe a cartoon → page 55 ► Karikaturen beschreiben, S. 214

a) **Describe and analyse the following cartoon by filling in suitable words from the box below.**

caption – cartoon – cartoonist – care – dangers – exaggerates – girl's – Internet – painting – past – publish – puzzled – sitting – social – users – waiting

"Don't worry, daddy already knows and likes you. He's hacked all your social media accounts."

The cartoon shows a living room in which we can see a table, a lamp and a [1.] ______ on the wall. Two young people – a girl and a boy – are [2.] ______ side by side on a sofa behind the coffee table. It looks as if it is the living room of the [3.] ______ parents. The girl is talking to the boy who looks a little [4.] ______. The boy seems to be at his girlfriend's home for the first time and he is [5.] ______ to see the girl's father or the girl's parents. According to the [6.] ______ the girl says: "Don't worry, daddy already knows and likes you. He's hacked all your social media accounts." The [7.] ______ is making fun of the situation. In the [8.] ______ parents did not know a lot about their daughter's or son's friends before they met them but today – regarding all the [9.] ______ networking accounts especially young people have – they can find out a lot more on the [10.] ______ beforehand. Of course, the cartoonist [11.] ______ but there is some truth in the cartoon because young people often [12.] ______ private data and pictures on the Internet which can be seen by other [13.] ______. I personally know some friends who do not [14.] ______ about their private data and so this cartoon can be a funny way to make them aware of the possible [15.] ______.

b) **Describe and analyse the following cartoon in a similar way. The words in the box may help you. Use a separate sheet of paper.**

caption – Wi-Fi (wireless Internet)

The cartoon shows …
The cartoonist is making fun of …
In my opinion …

"I've never eaten here. I come for the broadband."

E | Reading +

10 The Internet on the move

Complete the crossword below with words from pages 56 and 57 in your student's book.

ACROSS

4. opposite (often negative) side
8. having a feeling that you can do something well
9. become smaller
10. not relying on other people
12. program for a computer or smartphone
14. do the job of
15. like better

DOWN

1. in or to a foreign country
2. name the letters of a word in the right order
3. connected to the Internet
5. someone who does a job that requires a special skill
6. piece of work that must be done
7. holder of an academic diploma
9. not interesting
11. person who is paid to work for another person
13. give a job to someone

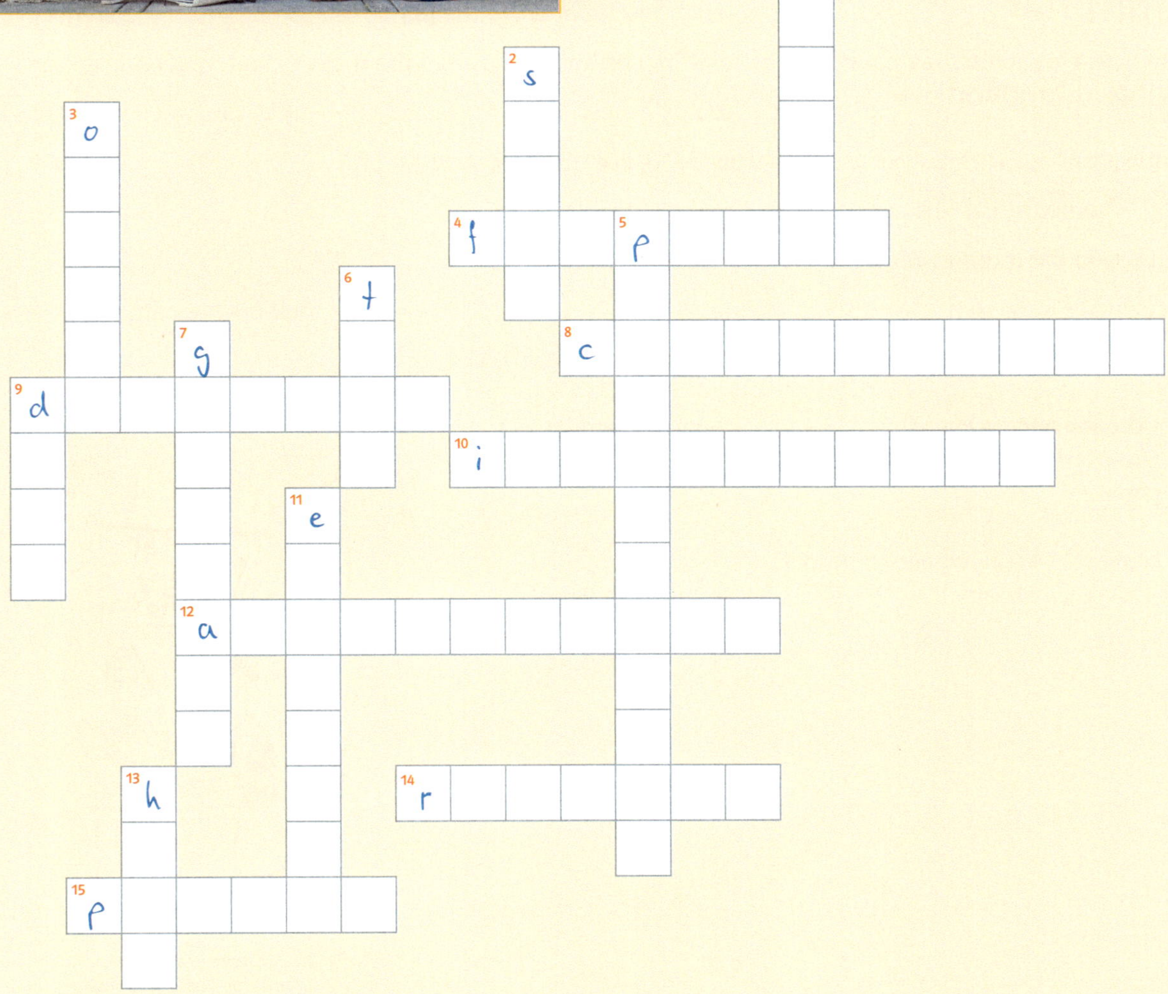

Unit 5

Social change

A | Getting started

1 Challenges of a changing society
→ pages 60 and 61 ► Vokabeln systematisch lernen, S. 238

Find the nouns for the following verbs.

1. to challenge ______
2. to head ______
3. to equal ______
4. to isolate ______
5. to employ ______
6. to apply ______
7. to reject ______
8. to communicate ______
9. to shift ______
10. to support ______
11 to govern ______
12. to balance ______

B | Grammar

2 Living in England
► Defining relative clauses, p. 182

Connect the sentence halves and add "who" or "which" to make defining relative clauses.

1. England is a country …	who which	a) sell cosmetics as well as medicine.
2. Beefeaters are guards …		b) work at the Tower of London.
3. Drugstores are shops …		c) died in a car accident.
4. Diana was a princess …		d) lies in the north of England.
5. Leeds is a big city …		**e) has a large number of immigrants.**

1. e) England is a country which has a large number of immigrants.
2. ______
3. ______
4. ______
5. ______

✗3 Changes at home

► Defining relative clauses, p. 182 ► Non-defining relative clauses, p. 183

Fill in "who" or "which" or leave out the relative pronoun.

According to a report [1.] , which was published by Clarks' Insurance last week the British are keeping more and more useless things in their homes. Many British homes are half full of stuff [2.] (which) people do not need or want any more. In the last fifty years rising incomes and technical developments have led to an increasing number of consumer goods [3.] which have found their way into our homes but they have not found their way out again. People especially keep electrical devices, clothes and toys because they think that one day they might be able to use them again. Dora Keegan, [4.] who is 43, is one of those people [5.] who knows that there are far too many things just lying around unused. Why can she not get rid of the things [6.] (which) she does not need any more?

"I've checked my house and found that there are computers, radios, bicycles, old clothes and children's toys. But how can I throw away things [7.] which cost hundreds of pounds? Nearly all the things [8.] which I found are still useable. There's the old doll [9.] , which belonged to my daughter, the bicycle [10.] which can be used by my grandchildren one day or the baby shoes [11.] (which) my mother kept for me. It seems very difficult to leave the past behind."

4 Rules at the National Women's History Museum

► Modal auxiliaries, p. 182

Complete the rules at the Women's History Museum.
Use "must" or "mustn't". mașânt (nicht dürfen)

1. **You [take] your bag into the museum.**
2. **You [leave] your bag in a locker.**
3. You **[turn]** your mobile phone off. întoarce
4. You **[use]** your mobile phone in the museum. utilizare
5. You **[be]** quiet. fi liniște
6. You **[shout or run]** in the museum. strigă sau fugi
7. You **[take]** photos in the museum. lua
8. You **[keep]** a safe distance between you and the pictures. a păstra
9. You **[touch]** the pictures. atingere
10. You **[smoke]** inside the building. fuma

1. You mustn't take your bag into the museum.
2. You must leave your bag in a locker.
3. You must your mobile phone off.
4. You mustn't use your mobile phone in the museum
5. You must be quiet.
6. You mustn't shout or run in the museum
7. You mustn't take photos in the museum
8. You must keep a safe distance between you and the pictures.
9. You mustn't touch the pictures.
10. You mustn't smoke inside the building.

5 Everything changes! What will life be like in 100 years' time?

► Modal auxiliaries, p. 182

Note down what you think the world will be like in 100 years' time. Use one of the expressions in the box.

(not) have to – (not) be allowed to – (not) be able to

Today …
1. **pupils must go to school.**
2. people can go skiing in the Alps.
3. Americans need not have an identity card.
4. a lot of older people cannot handle a computer.
5. guests must not smoke in restaurants.
6. people may drive cars with a petrol engine.
7. young people may drive a car at the age of 17.

Example:

1. In 100 years' time I think pupils will have to go to school, too. / Or: In 100 years' time I think pupils will not have to go to school any more.
2. In a 100 years' time, I think people will have the skill to ski in the Alps.
3. In a 100 years' time, I think Americans will not have to have an identity card.
4. In a 100 years' time, I think a lot of older people will be able to handle a computer
5. In a 100 years' time, I think guests will not be allowed to smoke in restaurants.
6. In a 100 years' time, I think people will be allowed to drive cars with a petrol engine.
7. In a 100 years' time, I think young people will not be able to drive a car at the age of 17.

6 Managing situations – Giving explanations and definitions

► Defining relative clauses, p. 182

Ein englischsprachiger Bekannter versteht einige deutsche Begriffe nicht. Erläutern Sie diese Begriffe unter der Verwendung von Relativsätzen.

1. Berufsschule
2. Fachhochschulreife
3. Klausur
4. Klassenbuch
5. Klassensprecher

1. Berufsschule is a college which …
2.
3.
4.
5.

C | Reading

7 Training skills – How to anticipate, skim and scan

► Antizipieren, Skimming, Scanning, S. 231

a) **Anticipating:**

1. Look at the photo and write down what you think the text may deal with.

   After looking at the photo I think the text may deal with ...

2. Look at the heading of the text and write down your ideas about the text.

   After reading the heading I think the text is about ...

b) **Skimming: Read the text below quickly to find out if your ideas in a)1. und a)2. were right. Tick the suitable box and give a reason for your answer.**

☐ My ideas about the text were right ...

☐ My ideas about the text were not right (because) ...

R c) **Scanning: Read the text again and find out about the facts in 1–8.**

HOW IT ALL DEVELOPED

Originally the Greek name for school meant "leisure". Today schools are institutions which pupils in most countries must attend. Formal schools have a long history: they existed in Greece and China more than 2,000 years ago. Islam was another culture which developed a school system. At first, children prayed and learned at mosques, but in the ninth century separate schools were introduced. In Europe during the Middle Ages schools mainly taught Latin. This led to the expression "grammar school", which still exists in Britain. But many children did not attend school because they had to work. It was only in 1880 that education for 5-to-10-year-old children became compulsory in Britain. In 1944 the school-leaving age was raised to 15 and schools were divided into primary and secondary schools. This is still the case today so pupils leave primary school at the age of 11. Many of the earlier schools in Europe and North America were one-room schools where one teacher taught pupils of all ages in the same classroom. From the 1920s on schools became larger institutions with several classrooms, offices, gyms and – in the past few decades – even computer labs.

1. The original meaning of the word "school" .... leisure
2. The age of the school system .... ______
3. The original place for children to learn in Islam .... ______
4. The subject pupils learned in the Middle Ages .... ______
5. "Grammar school" is a term that is still used in .... ______
6. The year in which all children had to go to school for the first time in Britain .. ______
7. The age at which pupils start going to secondary school in Britain .... ______
8. The number of classrooms in earlier schools .... ______

M d) **Sie bereiten eine Präsentation zum Thema „Schulen früher und heute" für Ihren Geschichtsunterricht vor. Entnehmen Sie die entsprechenden Informationen aus dem obenstehenden Artikel. Formulieren Sie ganze deutsche Sätze.** ► Mediation, S. 228

8 Carefree youth of today? ► Vokabeln systematisch lernen, S. 238

Make phrases – as they are used on pages 64 and 65 – by completing the verbs in the list below with words in the box.

about – about – about – at – for – from – out – out – out – through – up – up – with – with – with – with

1. to go ______
2. to be ______
3. to skim ______
4. to look ______
5. to point ______
6. to pick ______
7. to catch ______
8. to speak ______
9. to stress ______
10. to worry ______
11 to go ______
12. to cope ______
13. to suffer ______
14. to think ______
15. to match ______
16. to apply ______

9 ACADEMIC PERFORMANCE: top reason for teen stress → page 65

Fill in suitable phrases from task 8 to write a short summary of the text. Watch out for the correct tenses and forms.

The text "ACADEMIC PERFORMANCE: top reason for teen stress" [1.] ______ the problems of young people today. Lots of them are [2.] ______ their uncertain future and are [3.] ______ bad job perspectives. Increasing academic pressure often [4.] ______ them ______. Because of their financial problems many students have to do part-time jobs which makes it more difficult to [5.] ______ the academic work at college. As they do not want to lose social contact they often [6.] ______ with friends in the evening although there is little free time. One way to take time out from this stress is to [7.] ______ a voluntary activity in a foreign country – a so-called gap year.

D | Practice

10 Problems of the modern welfare state → page 66 ► Vokabeln systematisch lernen, S. 238

Some words often go together. Match the following words from list A with words from list B to make phrases as they are used in the listening text.

A

1. professor of ______
2. welfare ______
3. medical ______
4. pension ______
5. old-age ______
6. social ______
7. senior ______
8. family ______
9. National ______
10. unemployment ______
11. public ______
12. people in ______

B

a) treatment
b) pension
c) structure
d) economics
e) citizen
f) benefits
g) insurance
h) state
i) need
j) scheme
k) Health Service
l) services

11 Demographic developments: Multigenerational living → pages 66 / 67

Complete the table below with suitable words from the text.

1. ______________________

2. ______________________

3. ______________________

4. ______________________

5. ______________________

6. ______________________

7. ______________________

8. ______________________

9. ______________________

E | Reading +

12 Stay-at-home dads → page 69

Complete the crossword below and find the solution by filling in the corresponding English words from the text for their German equivalents.

1. primär, hauptsächlich
2. Kragen
3. Wachstum
4. Notwendigkeit
5. Abschluss
6. übereinstimmen, zusammentreffen mit
7. Kinderbetreuung
8. fördern, befördern
9. stetig
10. Beziehung, Zusammenhang
11. Karriere
12. Betreuer(in)
13. Armut
14. Durchschnitt

Solution

1.																	
2.																	
3.																	
4.																	
5.																	
6.																	
7.																	
8.																	
9.																	
10.																	
11.																	
12.																	
13.																	
14.																	

Unit B

Living in London

1 Showing the way

a) **You are standing at a bus stop close to Hungerford Bridge and ask a young woman for help. She tells you the way to Westminster Abbey. Choose six of the sentences below and put them in the right order to find the way.**

	A	Turn left into Horse Guards.		F	On your right you find the Houses of Parliament.
	B	Go down Victoria Embankment.		G	Turn right into Bridge Street.
	C	Turn left at the traffic lights.		H	Then you can see Westminster Abbey on your right.
	D	Go past Big Ben.		I	Go past Parliament Square.
	E	Take the Queen's Walk along the Thames.		J	Cross Westminster Bridge.

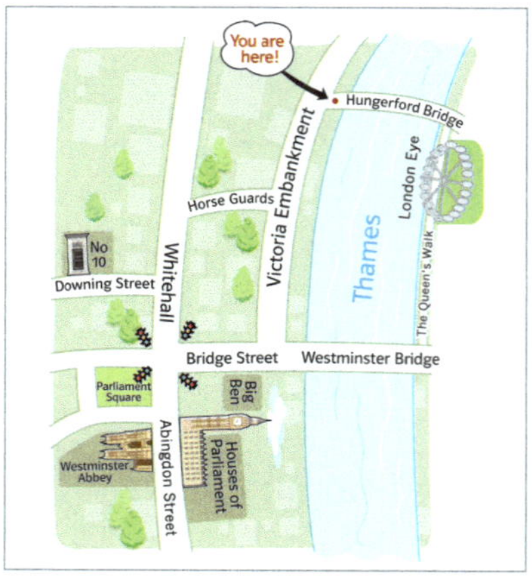

b) **After visiting Westminster Abbey you are in Abingdon Street close to Westminster Abbey now and ask a passer-by the way to the London Eye. Complete the following seven sentences so that it is easy to find the way. Use a separate sheet of paper.**

1. First go down ______________________
2. At the traffic lights …
3. Then go down …
4. Go past …
5. Cross …
6. After crossing …
7. Soon …

2 A new guest

Complete the following dialogue between a landlady of a guesthouse and a guest by filling in suitable words from the box.

call – else – easily – fine – from – I'm – may – meet – on – pleasant – pleased – serve – tired – welcome

Guest: Hello, I'm Frederik Smaland [1.] ______________ Sweden.

Landlady: [2.] ______________ to Southend Guesthouse, Frederik. [3.] ______________ Samantha Fox.

Guest: [4.] ______________ to meet you, Ms Fox.

Landlady: Nice to [5.] ______________ you, too. Please [6.] ______________ me Samantha. Did you have a [7.] ______________ journey?

Guest: I had no problems at all. The train arrived [8.] ______________ time and I found your guesthouse [9.] ______________.

Landlady: That's [10.] ______________. [11.] ______________ I show you your room now?

Guest: That would be nice. What time do you [12.] ______________ breakfast?

Landlady: From eight to nine. Is there anything [13.] ______________ I can do for you?

Guest: Thanks very much. I'm a bit [14.] ______________. I think I'll go to bed now. Good night.

3 At the breakfast table

a) **Match the parts of the questions in A and B with suitable answers in C and write their letters in the spaces behind the numbers.**

	▼	A		B		C
1.		May I	a)	come from, Rose?	i)	No, I've been staying here for a week.
2.		Have you	b)	to order?	j)	I'm from Cardiff. That's in Wales.
3.		Where do you	c)	just arrived?	k)	I'm going to do some sightseeing.
4.		What brings you to	d)	for breakfast, Graham?	l)	I would like to have a full English breakfast.
5.		What are	e)	join you?	m)	I'm doing a work placement here in London.
6.		And what are your plans for	f)	you doing here in London?	n)	Of course, please take a seat
7.		Are you ready	g)	this part of the world?	o)	I'm on holiday.
8.		What are you having	h)	the next few days?	p)	One moment, please.

b) Write the complete questions and answers. Use a separate sheet of paper.

4 British weather

Complete the crossword below by filling in suitable English words.

ACROSS

2. warm
4. heiß
7. frostig
9. sonnig
11. stürmisch
12. windig
14. kalt
15. diesig, trüb

DOWN

1. Regenschauer
3. regnerisch
5. unbeständig
6. bewölkt
8. Schnee
10. hell, klar
13. Nebel

Unit 6
Ecology

A | Getting started: We are all part of it!

1 Tackling climate change

→ page 76 ► Vokabeln systematisch lernen, S. 238

Some words often go together. Match the following words from list A with words from list B to make terms as they are used in the text.

A	▼			▼	
1.		greenhouse	7.		solar
2.		fossil	8.		carbon
3.		food	9.		weather
4.		global	10.		summer
5.		sun's	11.		CO_2
6.		degrees	12.		climate

B			
a)	emissions	g)	supply
b)	energy	h)	levels
c)	conditions	i)	Centigrade
d)	effect	j)	change
e)	footprint	k)	panel
f)	fuels	l)	temperatures

B | Grammar

2 Reporting what people said

► Reported speech, p. 189

Match the statements in reported speech with the corresponding statements in direct speech.

	▼	**Direct speech: Last week …**
1.	b	**Jonathan said: "I came here yesterday."**
2.		Lily and Emily said: "We don't know where he is."
3.		Oliver and Sue said: "We came here yesterday."
4.		Mohammed said to Cindy: "I like my new mobile phone."
5.		Gerald said to Lucy: "I like your new mobile phone."
6.		Sophie said: "I don't know where he is."
7.		Jill said: "I'm coming tomorrow."
8.		Olivia said: "I needn't do it."
9.		Daniel and Katie said: "We will discuss this topic tomorrow."

	Reported speech: He / she / they said (that) …
a)	she did not have to do it.
b)	**he had come there the day before.**
c)	she did not know where he was.
d)	she was coming the following day.
e)	they had come there the day before.
f)	he liked her new mobile phone.
g)	they would discuss that topic the following day.
h)	he liked his new mobile phone.
i)	they did not know where he was.

3 After a nature presentation ► Reported speech, p. 189

Derek took part in a nature presentation last week and now wants to tell his friends what the presenter said. Use the phrases below and write what Derek tells his friends.

This is part of the presentation:

"[1.] Welcome to my nature presentation! [2.] Thank you all for coming. [3.] Some days ago I was right here and I found this place ideal for the meeting today. [4.] I want to show you the beauty and the problems of our environment. [5.] This tree next to me is a good example. [6.] It has grown for many years. [7.] It is protecting us from the sunshine during the presentation. [8.] But it doesn't look as good as it did some years ago. [9.] Air pollution has made it difficult for many species to survive. [10.] Perhaps within only a few generations there will be no trees here any more. [11.] It is my aim to stop this development. [12.] I know that you are all here to help!"

(The presenter …) – said that – went on to say that – told us that – informed us that – stated that – added that – concluded that …

1. The presenter welcomed us to his nature presentation.
2. He thanked us all for coming.
3. The presenter said that some days before he had been right there and had …
4. He went on to say that …
5.
6.
7.
8.
9.
10.
11.
12.

4 GreenLife's FAQ-page ► Reported speech, p. 189

Report what the following visitors to GreenLife's home page wanted to know.

1 EmmaFX: **Has GreenLife already tried to help the panda?**

2 Drago21: **Where can I join the group?**

3 Drizzlezizzle: Did you take part in the latest demonstration for tuna?

4 Foxy1a: Is there a local group?

5 TreeTop: When did GreenLife become international?

6 EnviroTwo: Do you work together with other organizations?

7 LogoLogo: Where will the meeting take place next week?

8 DesmondDes: How much money do you get from companies?

9 Wishywashy: Are you also dealing with the water problems in the Third World?

1. EmmaFX wanted to know if GreenLife had already tried to help the panda.
2. Drago21 asked where he could / was able to join the group.
3.
4.
5.
6.
7.
8.
9.

5 Managing situations – Reporting a TV documentary ► Reported speech, p. 189

Sie haben im Fernsehen einen interessanten Film über die zukünftige Entwicklung unserer Erde gesehen. Die Wissenschaftler in dem Beitrag haben u. a. das Folgende gesagt:

1. „Wir haben neue Ergebnisse gefunden."
2. „Wir hoffen, dass wir in der Lage sein werden, der Umwelt zu helfen."
3. „Wir arbeiten gerade hart an den Problemen."
4. „Unsere Lösungen werden eine Menge Geld kosten."
5. „Wir haben vor einer Woche mit dem Präsidenten über unsere Pläne gesprochen."

Berichten Sie einem/r englischsprachigen Bekannten über das, was die Wissenschaftler gesagt haben.

1. The scientists stated that …
2.
3.
4.
5.

C | Reading: Where does our food come from?

6 You are what you eat → page 80 ► Vokabeln systematisch lernen, S. 238

Find the missing verbs or nouns for the following words in the text.

	Verb	Noun
1.		production
2.	to live	
3.	to consume	
4.	to develop	
5.	to compete	
6.		standard
7.		expectations
8.	to taste	

	Verb	Noun
9.	to react	
10.	to offer	
11.		contribution
12.	to pollute	
13.		modification
14.		label
15.	to protect	
16.	to challenge	

7 Training skills – How to work with a dictionary

► Mit dem Wörterbuch arbeiten, S. 234

a) **Put the words in the box into alphabetical order.**

economist – ecosystem – ecstatic – **ecological** – ecology – economic – economics – ecstasy – economy – ecologist – economical – economize

1. ecological
2. ______
3. ______
4. ______
5. ______
6. ______
7. ______
8. ______
9. ______
10. ______
11. ______
12. ______

b) **Look up the words in exercise a) in a dictionary and put them into the appropriate box below.**

Nouns	Adjectives	Verbs
economist		

c) **Look up the pronunciation of the words above and decide where to put the main stress (first, second or third syllable). Mark the syllable that is stressed.**

d) Look up the words in exercise a) in an English-English dictionary and match them with the following definitions.

1. ecological ______ concerning the relationships between plants, animals, people and their environment; causing minimal damage to the environment
2. ______ a person who studies the relationships between plants, animals, people and their environment; a person who specializes in ecology
3. ______ extreme feeling of great happiness; an illegal drug in pill form
4. ______ concerning the organization of the money, industry and trade of a country
5. ______ a person who studies, teaches or writes about economics
6. ______ the study of the production and consumption of goods and services in a society
7. ______ the organizational system or the management of the money, industry and trade of a country
8. ______ to save money by spending it carefully; to make economical use of sth., to avoid waste
9. ______ saving money or time or effort; not wasteful
10. ______ all of the plants and animals in a particular area and the complex relations between them and their environment; an ecological community together with its environment
11. ______ showing or feeling great happiness
12. ______ the study of relationships between plants, animals, people and their environment; the study of living things, their environment and the relations between them

e) Look up the words in exercise a) in a German-English dictionary and match the words with their German meanings.

1. Begeisterung, Ekstase ecstasy
2. Ökologie, Umweltschutz, Umweltforschung ______
3. sparsam, wirtschaftlich ______
4. Wirtschaft, Ökonomie ______
5. Wirtschaftswissenschaften, Wirtschaftslehre ______
6. verzückt, ekstatisch ______
7. Ökologe, Ökologin, Umweltschützer(in) ______
8. Ökosystem, Naturhaushalt ______
9. sparen, haushalten, sparsam wirtschaften ______
10. ökologisch, Umwelt- ______
11. ökonomisch, wirtschaftlich ______
12. Wirtschaftswissenschaftler(in), Volkswirt(in), Ökonom(in) ______

D | Practice

8 Consuming the world → page 82 ► Vokabeln systematisch lernen, S. 238

A2.11

a) **Put the following words from the listening task under a suitable heading.**

climate change – violence – supermarket – soil erosion – railway – trade – instability – flight – goods – lack of fresh water – road – products – overfishing – demand – conflict

Economy	Transportation	Ecological effects	Political effects

b) **Complete the list above with words that you remember from past tasks.**

E | Reading +: Saving nature

9 Earth has lost half its wildlife → page 85 ► Mit Texten ohne Wörterbuch umgehen, S. 232

Find suitable verbs in the text and put them in the correct box.

	Definition / Explanation	Verb
1.	divide into two equal parts	
2.	make unclean, contaminate	
3.	damage so badly that it cannot be repaired	
4.	supply, make available	
5.	defend, save, keep from being harmed	
6.	make, manufacture	
7.	get a general idea of the size, use mathematical processes	
8.	study closely and carefully	

	Definition / Explanation	Verb
9.	consume completely	
10.	move water from or to a particular place	
11.	send out, give off	
12.	take in sth. in a natural way	
13.	drop sharply	
14.	get rid of, leave rubbish	
15.	bring a product into a country	
16.	make certain, make sure	

Unit 7

The present and future of technology

A | Getting started: Cleaner energy

1 Scotland – fossil-free by 2030? → page 89 ► Vokabeln systematisch lernen, S. 238

Complete the following list with words which you can find in the text.

Fossil fuels	Renewable sources of energy	Energy sources available in and around Scotland

B | Grammar

2 Technology at home ► Passive voice, p. 191

What can or cannot be done? What must or must not be done? What should or should not be done? Make meaningful or funny sentences. Use the words from the boxes below. Use a separate sheet of paper.

1. **Bread**	keep	cooker
2. Milk	**toast**	laptop
3. Soup	write	dishwasher
4. Plates	make	**toaster**
5. E-mails	cook	telephone
6. Calls	clean	refrigerator

Example of a meaningful sentence:

Bread can be toasted in the toaster.

Example of a funny sentence:

Calls should not be made in the dishwasher.

3 How an easy chicken noodle soup is made

► Passive voice, p. 191

Write the steps below in the passive voice.

What you need for an easy chicken soup:
1 chicken, 3 large potatoes, 2 carrots, 200 g small noodles, 1 teaspoon salt, 2 pieces of chicken bouillon, 2 spoons dried or fresh parsley (Petersilie)

What must be done:
1. First clean the chicken under running water.
2. Then boil the chicken in 6 cups of salt water until the chicken is fully cooked.
3. Take the chicken out and cut it into pieces.
4. Peel the potatoes and cut them into small pieces.
5. Prepare the carrots in the same way.
6. Add chicken bouillon and cook the potatoes, carrots and chicken for twenty minutes.
7. At the end add the noodles and cook them until they are tender.
8. Decorate the soup with parsley.

1. First the chicken is cleaned under running water.
2. Then the chicken ...
3.
4.
5.
6.
7.
8.

4 Chocolate

► Passive voice, p. 191

In 1828 Van Houten [1.] **invented** the method of producing cocoa powder. He [2.] mixed this powder with sugar and [3.] made a drink that tasted delicious. Some years later an English company [4.] produced and sold the first chocolate bar. In 1875 a Swiss manufacturer [5.] made the first milk chocolate.

Today most people [6.] love chocolate. Last year chocolate lovers in the UK [7.] spent over 5 billion pounds. US consumers [8.] ate about half of the world's chocolate production. The Swiss eat the most chocolate per person – they [9.] consume more than 10 kg per person per year.

Rewrite the report about chocolate. Use the passive voice for the underlined verbs. Fill in the by-agent where necessary. Use a separate sheet of paper.

1. In 1828 the method of producing cocoa powder was invented by ...
2. This powder ...

5 Developments

► Passive voice, p. 191

a) **Match the following pictures with the inventions on the right.**

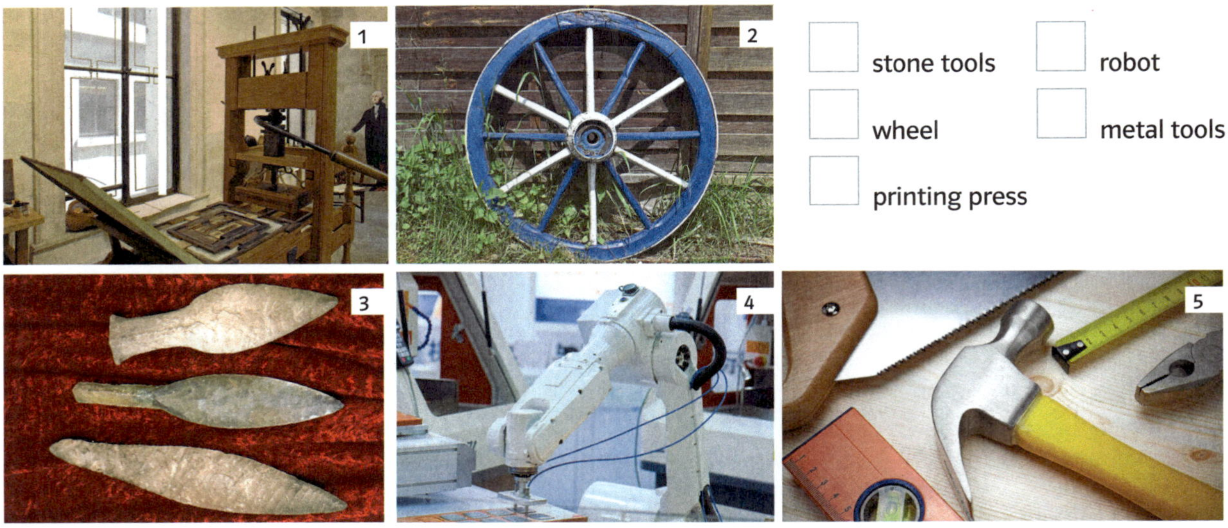

☐ stone tools ☐ robot
☐ wheel ☐ metal tools
☐ printing press

b) **Complete the following text by filling in a suitable form of the passive voice.**

In the beginning stone tools [**1. use**] were used. That is why this era [**2. call**] ______ the "Stone Age". At about that time, the use of fire [**3. discover**] ______. After metal tools [**4. invent**] ______ about 10,000 years ago many things became easier. The production of energy and transportation [**5. revolutionize**] ______ when the wheel [**6. invent**] ______ about 6,000 years ago. A big step forward [**7. make**] ______ when the printing press [**8. develop**] ______. In the last few hundred years our lives [**9. change**] ______ by many other important inventions. Today our work [**10. do**] ______ by robots and our children [**11. entertain**] ______ by TV or video games. Let us hope for the future that everyone's life [**12. make**] ______ more comfortable and safer by new inventions which [**13. cannot / even / think**] ______ of today.

6 Managing situations – Explaining regulations and notes

► Passive voice, p. 191

M

Sie werden von einem englischsprechenden Ausländer angesprochen, der wissen möchte, was die folgenden Inschriften auf Schildern bedeuten. Erläutern Sie diese unter der Verwendung des Passivs.

Example:

1. Credit cards are not accepted.
2. ______
3. ______
4. ______

C | Reading: Tidal lagoon power

7 Different views

► Mit Texten ohne Wörterbuch umgehen, S. 232

Match the following nouns from the texts on page 92 of your student's book with suitable definitions.

	▼	Noun from the text
1.		unemployment
2.		statement
3.		opportunity
4.		fuel
5.		tide
6.		resource
7.		turbine
8.		plant
9.		breakwater
10.		project
11.		emphasis
12.		impact

	Definition
a)	a good chance
b)	wall that is built out into the sea to protect a harbour or beach
c)	natural source of supply
d)	building or factory where s.th. is made
e)	engine with blades that are moved by wind or water
f)	the state of not having a job
g)	regular upward and downward movement of the level of the sea
h)	planned piece of work that has a specific purpose
i)	a powerful and often negative effect
j)	s.th. you say or write in a formal way – opinion that you express
k)	material that is burned to produce heat or power
l)	special importance or attention given to s.th.

D | Practice

8 Medical technology

► Mit Texten ohne Wörterbuch umgehen, S. 232

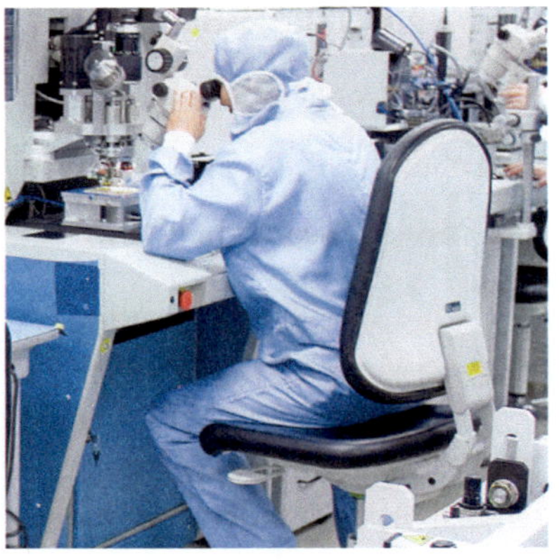

Complete the following composition about medical technology by filling in suitable words from the box below.

antibiotics – defects – defibrillators – diagnostics – diseases – gender – genetic – insemination – inventions – risks – X-rays

Medical technology has come a long way. A lot of [1.] ________________ and discoveries have helped to cure [2.] ________________ that were lethal years ago. [3.] ________________ help to examine the body, [4.] ________________ help to get people back into life and [5.] ________________ keep people alive who would have died from infections a hundred years ago.

Today there is a lot of discussion going on about the pros and cons of [6.] ________________ engineering. Artificial [7.] ________________ has helped millions of men and women to have a baby. With the help of pre-implantation [8.] ________________ doctors can test embryos for genetic [9.] ________________. On the other hand, it can also be used for choosing the [10.] ________________ or the size of a baby. This is, however, illegal in many countries. Nobody really knows where this development will lead us to – it seems there is no limit to the technical development in the future – with all its chances and [11.] ________________.

9 Training skills – How to write a composition

a) **"Modern technology does not really make life better." Underline the arguments below in two different colours. Use green for arguments for and red for arguments against modern technology.**

- creates new jobs
- replaces workers with computers and robots
- makes work more efficient
- makes hard work easier with the help of machinery
- lets machines do the dirty and dangerous work
- increases unemployment
- increases international competitiveness
- connects people worldwide through information technology and new or faster forms of transport
- has led to weapons of mass destruction
- access to information is easier
- uses a lot of energy
- communication has become cheaper, quicker and more efficient
- developing countries cannot afford advanced technology
- people in developing countries are still dying of hunger
- people must learn new skills for the new production methods
- makes life easier
- medical science saves lives
- it is becoming more and more complex and difficult to handle

b) **Choose those three arguments for and against modern technology that you think are the most important.**

c) **Copy the following table into your exercise book and write your composition.**

Heading
Modern technology does not really make life better

Introduction
We are all surrounded by modern technology today. We work on computers, communicate by Internet or mobile phone and can watch football matches on TV that are taking place right now thousands of miles away. This …

Arguments against / for the statement
Some people argue that …
On the other hand …

Your point of view
I think …
In conclusion I would like to …

1. Complete the introduction.
2. Use the arguments that you have chosen in b) and write them down in complete sentences. First write down arguments which do not correspond to your opinion. Then state the arguments which express your opinion. Use connectives from the first *Help* box in your student's book on page 93.
3. In conclusion, state your opinion. Use phrases from the second *Help* box on page 93.
4. Check what you have written.

E | Reading +: Genetically-modified food

10 There is no choice

Complete the crossword below by filling in words from pages 96 and 97 in your student's book. The first letters have already been given.

ACROSS

2. wahrscheinlich
3. Mangel
5. Verlass, Zutrauen
9. Dekade, Zeitraum von 10 Jahren
10. Herausforderung
16. Wissenschaft
18. Produktivität
21. Pflanze
22. Planet
23. verändert, modifiziert
24. Forscher
25. Milliarde

DOWN

1. drängen
2. Pestizid
4. erörtern, debattieren
6. Hungern, Verhungern
7. Veränderung
8. genetisch
11. leiden
12. Kultivierung, Anbau
13. nachhaltig
14. inakzeptabel
15. Bevölkerung
17. Saat, Feldfrucht, Getreide
19. Nutzen, Vorteil
20. Antwort, Reaktion
21. (leistungs-)stark, mächtig

Unit 8

The service industry

A | Getting started

1 Careers in tourism and leisure

→ page 101 ► Mit Texten ohne Wörterbuch umgehen, S. 232

Fill in the gaps of the following summary with suitable words from the text.

While other people are going on holidays in the summer people working in the [1.] ______________ and [2.] ______________ industry experience a busy time. Many new jobs have been created in this business area so there are many [3.] ______________ to find work today. Working in the tourism industry can give you the chance to [4.] ______________ to far-away countries but there is also a wide [5.] ______________ of jobs in England. When you apply for a job it could be helpful to have a university [6.] ______________ or if you already have some job [7.] ______________ in the tourism industry but most of all new employees must have excellent [8.] ______________ [9.] ______________. They must always be aware that tourists come [10.] ______________.
Pawan Durani thinks that a job in the tourism industry is very [11.] ______________ and can be much [12.] ______________. He has already visited the Far [13.] ______________ and Central America and has got to know a lot of typical tourist [14.] ______________ all over the world. He believes that the practical training is just as important as the [15.] ______________ he has learnt on several courses.

B | Grammar

2 Too late?

► Conditionals, p. 190

The Barker family are going on a trip to Majorca tomorrow. Write down in complete sentences what will happen to them if they do or do not do certain things. Use the phrases in the order given and watch out for the tenses.

1. alarm clock does not ring
2. the Barkers get up late
3. they are in a hurry
4. they forget their passports
5. they are not able to check in at the airport
6. the Barkers decide to drive home to get their passports
7. they are not in time for their flight
8. they spend their holidays in England
9. they do not have as much sunshine
10. the children do not get sunburned
11. they do not suffer from skin problems when they are older

1. If the alarm clock does not ring, the Barkers will get up late.
2. If the Barkers get up late, they will be ...
3.
4.
5.
6.
7.
8.
9.
10.

So it will be better for the Barker family if the alarm clock does not ring in the morning.

3 What would happen if ... ? ► Conditionals, p. 190

Make if-sentences as in the example.

1. **rain / not play badminton**
   If it rained, I would not play badminton.
2. have money / buy a car
3. be sick / not go on holidays
4. (Toby) like football / watch it on TV
5. (Mandy) go on holiday to the USA / visit the White House
6. (Roberta and Sue) live in London / go shopping a lot
7. (Dave and Allen) go to Ireland / travel by ferry
8. (Vance) have a driving licence / go by motorbike

4 Transport in the past and in the future

► Conditionals, p. 190

a) **Match suitable parts of the following sentences.**

1.	c	**If Columbus's ship had sunk,**	a)	if – you – not start – now
2.		If someone invents a very fast spaceship,	b)	driving – be – less dangerous
3.		The oil reserves would last longer	c)	**he – not discover – America**
4.		If people drove more slowly,	d)	if – Gottlieb Daimler – not have – the idea
5.		Fewer people would travel by plane	e)	if – cars – consume – less petrol
6.		Someone else would have invented the car	f)	if – flights – be – more expensive
7.		Columbus would not have been able to search for India	g)	we – be able – travel – to other galaxies
8.		There would be more road accidents	h)	if – the Queen – not give – him the money
9.		You will never reach your aim	i)	if – people – buy – more cars

b) **Write the above parts in complete sentences. Watch out for the different tenses.**

1. If Columbus's ship had sunk, he wouldn't have discovered America.
2.
3.
4.
5.
6.
7.
8.
9.

5 Managing situations – Going to the USA

► Conditionals, p. 190

Sie wollen eine Reise in die USA machen und übermitteln in einem Internet-Chat einem amerikanischen Freund einige Informationen, die Ihnen eine Mitarbeiterin im Reisebüro gegeben hat. Benutzen Sie dabei „if"-Sätze.

1. **„Sie werden im Internet einchecken können, wenn Sie Zeit sparen wollen."**
2. „Wenn Sie im Hotel frühstücken wollen, werden Sie zusätzlich $10 bezahlen müssen."
3. „Wenn Sie mit einem Partner verreisten, würde die Reise billiger für Sie sein."
4. „Wenn Sie vor einer Woche gekommen wären, hätte ich ein besonderes Angebot gehabt."
5. „Sie werden $300 mehr bezahlen müssen, wenn Sie direkt nach Washington fliegen wollen."

1. I will be able to check in via Internet if I want to save time.
2. If I want ...
3.
4.
5.

C | Reading: Mass tourism

6 Training skills – How to answer questions on a text

a) **Find out which tenses are used in the following questions.**

	Question	Tenses	Answer
1.	**Where did the Waltons travel last year?**	past simple	**Hawaii**
2.	Where do many Germans usually spend their holidays?		Germany
3.	When did the President visit India?		two months ago
4.	Where will you go at Christmas?		Austria
5.	What countries have been popular in the past few years?		Spain, France
6.	Where had the Prime Minister been before he went to Canada? (2 tenses)		Alaska
7.	Where was his wife staying at that time?		10 Downing Street
8.	Why are the holiday makers leaving?		because of the rain

b) **Answer the questions above in complete sentences. Be careful about the tenses. Use a separate sheet of paper.**

1. The Waltons travelled to Hawaii last year.

7 It's not only sunshine and fun → page 104

Fill in the crossword puzzle with suitable English words which you find in the text.

ACROSS

6. behandeln
7. Reserven
8. Verbraucher
10. Einnahmen
12. beitragen
13. Risiko
16. Umwelt
17. Erwärmung
19. Emission, Ausstoß
20. Grundwasser
22. Saison
23. unterstützen
24. Entfernung

DOWN

1. benötigen
2. Urlaubsort
3. Wirkung, Effekt
4. Reiseziel
5. Attraktion
9. verschmutzen, vergiften
11. Brunnen
14. Knappheit
15. gewaltig, enorm
18. (Umwelt-) Verschmutzung
21. Regen

D | Practice

8 Fitness and health

► Vokabeln systematisch lernen, S. 238

a) **Complete the word families. Fill in suitable nouns for the adjectives and verbs in the table.**

b) **Find out which ending could fit for each of the groups of nouns.**

	Adjective	Noun
1.	fit	
2.	well	
3.	busy	
4.	happy	
	Common ending for these nouns?	

	Adjective	Noun
5.	sustainable	
6.	responsible	
7.	popular	
8.	active	
	Common ending for these nouns?	

	Verb	Noun
9.	to treat	
10.	to manage	
11.	to employ	
12.	to equip	
	Common ending for these nouns?	

	Verb	Noun
13.	to operate	
14.	to inform	
15.	to educate	
16.	to rehabilitate	
	Common ending for these nouns?	

E | Reading+: Serving people

9 Living on $2.13 an hour

→ page 108 ► Mit Texten ohne Wörterbuch umgehen, S. 232

Find synonyms for the following words or expressions in the text. Note down the line in which you have found the synonym.

1. the money that you get for working – ____________________ (line ....)
2. things that you can eat – ____________________ (line ....)
3. every day – ____________________ (line ....)
4. people who buy things – ____________________ (line ....)
5. money that you have to pay for living in a flat – ____________________ (line ....)
6. remember – ____________________ (line ....)
7. per hour – ____________________ (line ....)
8. in reality – ____________________ (line ....)
9. curriculum vitae (CV) – ____________________ (line ....)
10. rise – ____________________ (line ....)

Unit C

Working in London

1 Introducing people

Fill in the gaps in the following bubbles with words from the box.

come – from – introduce – meet –
myself – name – pleased – this

1. Nice to ________________ you.
2. Let me ________________ you to Mr Conrad.
3. Ms Davids, ________________ is Susan Doyle.
4. ________________ to meet you.
5. Let me introduce ________________.
6. My ________________ is Mel.
7. Where are you ________________?
8. I ________________ from Bristol.

2 Showing people around

Look at the plan of the hotel on page 113 of your student's book and complete the following description with suitable words from the box.

in front – next – behind – between – the left – far – the back

1. The reception is right ________________ the entrance.
2. The reception is ________________ of the general office.
3. The general office is ________________ the toilets and the personnel manager's office.
4. The bar is ________________ to the lounge.
5. The general manager's office is not ________________ away from the executive suite.
6. You'll find the kitchen at ________________ of the hotel.
7. You can see the restaurant over there on ________________.

3 Making arrangements on the phone

Put the following parts of the telephone calls into the correct order.

1.

	A	I'd like to speak to Susan Atkins.
	B	Peter Jones speaking.
	C	Grand Tour Hotel. How can I help you?
	D	Thanks.
	E	Who's calling, please?
	F	Just a moment, Mr Jones. I'll put you through.

2.

	A	Thanks, I'm fine.
	B	Hello Susan. This is Richard.
	C	What can I do for you, Richard?
	D	Susan Atkins.
	E	Hello Richard. Nice to hear from you again. How are you?
	F	Well, I wonder if it is possible to arrange a meeting for next week.

3.

	A	Well, I'm out on Tuesday morning. Could you manage Tuesday afternoon?
	B	What about next Tuesday?
	C	That suits me, too. I look forward to seeing you then.
	D	Just a moment. Let me get my diary – you said Tuesday?
	E	Right. Would Tuesday morning be OK?
	F	Yes, Tuesday afternoon would suit me fine. Shall we say three o'clock?

4 Helping people

Some of the guests in your hotel need help or advice. Match their requests with suitable answers.

		Guest's request
	A	Could you make a copy for me?
	B	I need a taxi.
	C	Do you have Wi-Fi here?
	D	I'd like to visit the National Museum afterwards.
	E	I need to wash my hands.

	Your answer
F	No problem. Just take the second door on the right.
G	It's a free service for our guests. The code is DX-5439gH.
H	Yes, of course. I'll call Jason to do that for you.
I	Just a moment. I'll call one for you.
J	I can really recommend that. I'll show you the way then.

Unit 9

Living and working in a globalized world

A | Getting started: Migrant workers

1 What's your story? → page 117 ► Mit Texten ohne Wörterbuch umgehen, S. 232

Match the following words from the comments with their explanations by connecting them with lines.

	Word from the text
1.	benefits
2.	expatriate (expat)
3.	national insurance contributions
4.	prejudice
5.	nationality
6.	accent
7.	skin
8.	tax
9.	immigrate

	Explanation
a)	status of being a member of a particular nation
b)	money which you pay to the state to receive a pension at old age and other benefits
c)	a feeling of dislike for a person or group of people because of their race, sex or religion
d)	come to a country to live there
e)	the natural outer covering of the body of a person or animal
f)	a charge on persons or property which has to be paid to the government for public purposes
g)	money that is paid by the government when someone becomes sick or stops working
h)	person (mostly British or American) who leaves their country to live/work in another one (often for a certain time period)
i)	way of pronouncing words which is typical for people in a particular region or country

B | Grammar

2 A meeting of a One World group ► Infinitive, p. 191

Desmond Truly took part in an information evening held by a local One World group last night. At home he tells his parents what the speaker, Mrs Wilson, said. Report Desmond's statements and use one of the verbs from the box below.

want – make – expect – ask – advise – tell – let

1. **"Inform as many people as possible about our group."**
2. "Don't leave the poor countries alone with their problems."
3. "Think about the ways you can help."
4. "Please come to our next meeting."

5. "Let's watch the new film about Central Africa."
6. "Don't look the other way when there are people in need."
7. "Please have a cup of tea in the break."
8. "Help with our future activities, please."

1. Mrs Wilson wanted us to inform as many people as possible about their group.
2. She asked us not to ...
3. She made us ...
4. ______
5. ______
6. ______
7. ______
8. ______

3 What do you prefer? ► Gerund, p. 192

At the weekend Desmond went to the One World shop because he wanted to offer his help. He met Debbie, who had already been working there for some years.

In their conversation about their hobbies and interests Desmond mentioned the following things. Write about Desmond. Use the words in brackets.

1. **"It's nice to watch films on TV." [like]**
   Desmond likes watching films on TV.
2. "I don't really think that basketball is interesting to watch." **[dislike]**
   ______
3. "I like my skates but I like my bike even better." **[prefer]**
   ______
4. "I can't stand those people who have nothing to do. I don't want to just hang around." **[hate]**
   ______
5. "It's nice to talk to you, Debbie." **[enjoy]**
   ______
6. "I really want to help other people and I enjoy that very much." **[love]**
   ______

4 Helping at the One World shop ► Gerund, p. 192

a) **Complete the following phrases with a suitable preposition from the box.**

at – for – of – of – of – of – in – in – to

1. **be afraid** of
2. have the chance ______
3. be good ______
4. look forward ______
5. succeed ______
6. have the opportunity ______
7. be tired ______
8. apologize ______
9. have difficulty ______

b) **This is what Debbie said when she met Desmond at the shop. Rewrite her statements. Use the phrases in exercise a).**

1. **We can change the world a little.**
   We have the chance (opportunity) of changing the world a little.
2. Sometimes it is not easy for us to find new members. ______
3. I don't want to make too many mistakes. ______
4. We managed to raise £800 at the last meeting. ______
5. I think in July we'll have a nice barbecue. ______
6. I am sorry if I talk too much. ______

C | Reading: Profits or ethics?

5 Working conditions

► Mit Texten ohne Wörterbuch umgehen, S. 232

Fill in the following summary about working conditions in the textile industry with one of the adjectives or adverbs in the box.

cheap(ly) – inadequate(ly) – invisible(-bly) – large(ly) – legal(ly) – poor(ly) – proper(ly) – real(ly)

Thousands of sewing machines can be heard again in workshops around Britain but the workers cannot be seen: they are [1.] ______ to the public because they work in backyards. About 12,000 workers, mostly women, are employed in this sector and are not [2.] ______ paid – they only receive three pounds an hour or even less. The working conditions are [3.] ______ bad, they are [4.] ______ for a developed country. Of course, paying less than the minimum wage is not [5.] ______ but many women from Asia or Eastern Europe only speak English [6.] ______. So this is their only chance to contribute to their household income. Companies want to save money so they are interested in producing as [7.] ______ as possible. And their workers pay the price, a problem that is [8.] ______ common not only in Britain, but also in other European countries and beyond.

6 £3 per hour! A fair deal?

→ page 120

Complete the following lists with words from the text.

1. **People:** a) empl______ b) fas______ des______ c) res______ d) wom______ e) chil______
2. **Organizations and businesses:** a) tex______ ind______ b) comp______ c) gar______ ind______ d) ret______

3. **Conditions:** a) hea_______ and saf_______ sta_______ b) bul_______ c) toi_______ bre_______ d) empl_______ cont_______ e) work_______ rig_______
4. **Money:** a) wa_______ b) mat_______ pa_______ c) lab_______ co_______ d) inc_______
5. **Buildings and machinery:** a) fac_______ b) sh_______ c) works_______ d) sew_______ mac_______

7 Training skills – How to do mediation exercises ► Mediation, S. 228

Sie haben die Aufgabe, für Ihren Unterricht einen Vortrag über Bangladesch auf Deutsch vorzubereiten. Sie haben in einer Internet-Enzyklopädie den folgenden Text gefunden.

a) **Ordnen Sie dem Text über Bangladesch diese Überschriften zu.**

Regierungssystem – Wirtschaft – Bevölkerung – Geografie – Geschichte

Bangladesh

A _______________

Bangladesh is a country in South Asia. It is surrounded by India in the west, north and east and by Myanmar in the east. Bangladesh opens to the Bay of Bengal in the south, which leads into the Indian Ocean. The country covers an area of 56,977 square miles, which is less than half the size of Germany. Most parts are less than 12 m above sea level – most of the land is flat and very fertile. Bangladesh is also called the land of rivers.

B _______________

For hundreds of years the area called Bengal belonged to the British Empire. From the beginning of the 20th century on there was a call for independent states there. After World War II the western part of Bengal became part of India and the eastern part had to join Pakistan. After a civil war Bangladesh declared its independence in 1971.

C _______________

Today, Bangladesh, which is officially called the People's Republic of Bangladesh, is a parliamentary democratic state. Its capital is Dhaka. After some unrest following independence Sheik Hasina became Prime Minister and head of government for the third time in 2014 in a largely fair election.

D _______________

In the last 50 years the population of Bangladesh has doubled. Now the country has more than 150 million inhabitants, which makes it 8th in the world by population. As the country is relatively small this means that Bangladesh is one of the most densely populated countries. The official language is Bengali while English is used as a second language. The vast majority (about 85%) of Bangladeshi are Muslims.

E _______________

Bangladesh is a developing country. Its currency is the Taka. Bangladesh is still an important agricultural producer with emphasis on rice, tea, jute and fruit. The industrial sector includes the textile industry which makes up 70% of the country's export earnings. But all in all Bangladesh is a poor country. With only a few thousand dollars income per person it is about the 150th "richest" nation in the world. About 25% of the population still live below the international poverty line, which means that people live on less than US$1.25 per day.

b) **Markieren Sie in den jeweiligen Abschnitten die wichtigsten Informationen.**

c) **Sammeln Sie in Ihrem Heft diese Stichpunkte auf Deutsch unter den fünf vorgegebenen Überschriften als Grundlage für Ihren Vortrag über Bangladesch.**

D | Practice

8 Globalization ► Vokabeln systematisch lernen, S. 238

Find suitable verbs or nouns for the following words.

	Verb	Noun
1.	to grow	
2.		production
3.	to export	
4.		sale
5.	to demand	
6.		attention
7.	to state	
8.		commitment
9.	to protect	
10.		existence
11.	to shop	
12.		improvement

	Verb	Noun
13.	to dress	
14.		label
15.	to change	
16.		trainers
17.	to enable	
18.		globalization
19.	to organize	
20.		cooperation
21.	to communicate	
22.		movement
23.	to manage	
24.		costs

E | Reading +: We are the change!

9 Not all Asian clothing factories are unethical → page 124

Complete the crossword on the opposite page by filling in English words from the text.

ACROSS

2. örtlich, lokal
5. Armut
7. nützlich
9. Missbrauch
11. Nachhaltigkeit
15. Fußabdruck
17. Rohstoff, Bodenschatz
18. Bekleidung

DOWN

1. Fabrik, Mühle
3. Baumwolle
4. Ausbeutung
5. Herstellung, Produktion
6. Anforderungen
8. Kunde
10. Mode
12. Wohltätigkeit (sorganisation)
13. Kollege, Kollegin
14. Unglück
16. benötigen, fordern
19. behandeln

10 Managing situations – Writing a blog in English

► Infinitive, p. 191 ► Gerund, p. 192

Sie schreiben ein internationales Blog auf Englisch, in dem Sie auch andere Menschen überzeugen wollen, dass sie etwas für eine gerechtere Welt tun können. Schreiben Sie auf Englisch, dass …

1. **es Ihnen gefällt, im 21. Jahrhundert zu leben.**
2. Sie nun die Chance haben, viele Menschen zu informieren.
3. Sie nicht wollen, dass die Menschen in der Dritten Welt an Hunger leiden.
4. Sie darum bitten, Fairtrade-Produkte zu kaufen.
5. Sie sich darauf freuen, vielen Kindern damit zu helfen.
6. der Gedanke daran Sie auf eine bessere Welt hoffen lässt.

1. I enjoy living in the 21st century.
2. ______
3. ______
4. ______
5. ______
6. ______

Unit 10

International organizations and politics

A | Getting started: Our needs and our rights

1 Are we all born equal and free? → page 129 ► Vokabeln systematisch lernen, S. 238

Fill in suitable words from list B to make meaningful expressions in list A. You can find these expressions in the text.

	A		B
1.	human ✓ ...	a)	Human Rights
2.	international	b)	states
3.	Declaration of	c)	agreements
4.	United	d)	speech
5.	member	e)	the law
6.	political	f)	organizations
7.	freedom of	g)	rights
8.	equality before	h)	education
9.	right to	i)	Nations
10.	social	j)	participation
11.	non-governmental	k)	International
12.	Amnesty	l)	security

B | Grammar

2 Life in Nicaragua ► Participle, p. 192

Read the following report by Rita, a young woman working in Nicaragua. Replace the underlined phrases in the report. Use the present or past participle.

I have lived in the country [1.] <u>which is officially called the Republic of Nicaragua</u> for three years now. It is the largest country in Central America. The region [2.] <u>which lies close to the Caribbean Sea</u> is my favourite part of the country. One quarter of the population [3.] <u>that lives in Nicaragua</u> lives in Managua – the capital of Nicaragua. Most of the population, [4.] <u>which totals nearly six million</u>, speaks Spanish. In 1502 Columbus was the first European to reach this region. In the 16th century the Spanish founded some important towns here but most of the Indian civilization, [5.] <u>which was destroyed by</u>

the Spanish, has disappeared. Today Nicaragua is independent. Many people here are rather poor. There is a high unemployment rate and those [6.] who have jobs only earn little money. Food is cheap, but products [7.] which are made in the USA cost even more than there. A pair of jeans costs 30% more than in the US! Nevertheless, the cost of living for me is very low and there is a lot I like about Nicaragua. Tourists and people [8.] who live here can enjoy fresh food and great beaches. Politics, on the other hand, is always a problem here.

1. I have lived in the country officially called the Republic of Nicaragua for three years.
2. The region lying close to the Caribbean Sea is my favourite part of the country.
3. One quarter of the population ______
4. Most of the population ______
5. Most of the Indian civilization ______
6. There is a high unemployment rate and those ______
7. Food is cheap, but products ______
8. Tourists and people ______

3 Getting to know Nicaragua

► Participle, p. 192

A lot of things happened to Rita after moving to Nicaragua. Join the pairs of sentences and use the present participle.

1. Rita heard a lot about Nicaragua. Then she decided to live there.
   After hearing a lot about Nicaragua Rita decided to live there.
2. She wanted to know as much as possible about Nicaragua. So she did a lot of research into the country.
   Wanting to know ...
3. She went to Nicaragua. Before that she sold her car.
   Before ______
4. She looked for a place to live for a few days. Then she rented a small house.
   After ______
5. Rita worked for a US company first. She met a lot of US Americans.
   While ______
6. She is very open-minded. So she soon found friends in Nicaragua.
   ______
7. She wanted to get to know the country better. So Rita bought an old motorbike.
   ______
8. She has had so many nice experiences in Nicaragua. So Rita wants to stay there forever.
   After ______

4 Humanitarian help for the Third World

► Infinitive, p. 191 ► Gerund, p. 192

Complete the following text. Fill in the infinitive with or without "to", the gerund or a participle of the verbs in brackets.

Your help is needed!

After **[1. lose]** losing their homes, about 300,000 Tamils are at present living in the worst possible conditions. One of the reasons **[2. cause]** ______ these conditions at the moment is the conflict with the government in Sri Lanka. However, heavy rain and floods have also made the Tamils **[3. leave]** ______ their homes. Many people suffer from malaria and other illnesses are increasing, too. The refugees are very poor and need urgent help. After **[4. be attacked]** ______ by different militant groups, most international aid groups have left the conflict area for safety reasons. As the government is not interested in **[5. help]** ______ the refugees there are only some local groups left **[6. try]** ______ to help, but they need our assistance.

That is why we want to make people **[7. join]** ______ our action day on 8 October. We are asking you **[8. come]** ______ to our information evening on the night before. You have the opportunity of **[9. offer]** ______ help in the way you can do best. Maybe you are good at **[10. collect]** ______ money or you want to assist us at our information desk. Perhaps you are good at **[11. create]** ______ home pages? We must all be interested in **[12. provide]** ______ a minimum standard of living for everyone. We still enjoy **[13. live]** ______ in peace but this can change when there is trouble around us. Let us **[14. help]** ______ other people and in a way we can also do something for ourselves and for our children at the same time.

5 Managing situations – Creating a homepage for your One-World-Group

► Infinitive, Gerund, Participle pages 191 / 192

Sie gestalten die Homepage Ihrer Eine-Welt-Gruppe in Deutsch und in Englisch. Übertragen Sie in Ihrem Heft den folgenden deutschen Text ins Englische.

Hallo!
Hast du keine Lust mehr, deine Abende vor dem Fernseher zu verbringen? Hast du Interesse daran, mit jungen Leuten zusammenzuarbeiten? Hilfst du gerne anderen Leuten, denen es finanziell weniger gut geht als dir oder die gesundheitliche Probleme haben? Wenn die Antworten auf diese Fragen „ja" sind, dann werde Mitglied in unserer Eine-Welt-Gruppe. Bei regelmäßigen Treffen wirst Du allen möglichen jungen Leuten begegnen. Außerdem hast Du die Möglichkeit, Mitglieder von Gruppen aus anderen Ländern kennenzulernen.

C | Reading: Human rights and mass surveillance

6 Training skills – How to write a material-based composition

→ page 104 ► Materialgestützter Aufsatz, S. 199

a) **As violence and vandalization happen more often at schools, authorities are considering an increased use of security measures. Describe the current situation at schools and discuss the benefits and disadvantages of increasing security measures. Finally state your point of view. Before you write the composition do tasks a – e on the materials given.**
Read the following text carefully. The main facts and arguments have already been underlined for you. Rewrite them on the lines on the right. Use your own words.

A school police officer might have saved Bailey Gwynne, says expert

John Carnochan, one of the UK's most senior violence reduction experts, is clear: if there had been a police officer based at Cults academy in October, Bailey Gwynne may not have died. The fatal stabbing of the Aberdeen schoolboy […] has inevitably led to calls for school security to be tightened and accusations that warning signs were missed. Carnochan […] who co-founded *Police Scotland's* pioneering violence reduction unit (VRU) in 2005, […] says: "My instinct would be that if there had been a campus cop at Cults, they would have picked up on the animosity and isolation of the offender. Because their job is to establish a good relationship with the kids […]."

The VRU […] originally piloted "campus cops" – police officers physically based in a cluster of nearby primaries and secondary schools – in Aberdeen more than a decade ago. There are now about 80 peppered across Scotland. […]

Linzie Foster, a bright and energetic constable with two teenagers of her own, has been based at Whitehill secondary school in the east end of Glasgow for four years. […]

"These are kids who, if they had a different background, their lives would be very different – sometimes these kids don't have anyone to tell them that their behaviour is wrong," she says. Foster adds carefully: "Some of the families are not immediately pro-police in the east end of Glasgow. So this is about relationship building." […]

Foster has seen significant changes in this area, where the VRU began its targeting interventions in gang culture a decade ago: "Gang fighting has gone right down and there's an understanding that getting a conviction for carrying a knife can have a major impact on your future," she says. […]

(297 words)

Quelle: Libby Brooks, *The Guardian*, www.theguardian.com, March 15, 2016.

a. Example:

John Carnochan, a British expert on violence reduction, points out that police officers stationed at schools might prevent violence there. …

b. ____________________

c. ____________________

d. ____________________

e. ____________________

b) Read the text "Schule unter Spionageverdacht" carefully. Then look at the underlined arguments and write down their content in English.

Schule unter Spionageverdacht

Ein moderner Schüler schreibt nicht mehr mit gespitztem Bleistift von der Tafel ab. Er tippt die Formeln und Vokabeln gleich in seinen Laptop. Und ein moderner Lehrer? Der hält nicht mehr Wache auf dem Pausenhof und ermahnt mal hier einen Rüpel und tröstet da einen Außenseiter. Er setzt sich lieber ins Lehrerzimmer, schaltet sich unbemerkt per *Remote Desktop*, also per Fernzugriff auf den Laptop seines Schülers, aktiviert ebenso heimlich Webcam und Mikrofon, und beobachtet dann das wilde Treiben seines Schützlings. Der übrigens schon längst zu Hause ist. […]

Was wie eine überzogene Neuauflage alter Überwachungsängste klingt, scheint laut dem *Courthouse News Service*, einem amerikanischen Nachrichtendienst für Anwälte, tatsächlich so passiert zu sein. Die Verwaltung der Harrington High-School in Pennsylvania hat ihren Schülern offensichtlich nicht nur tragbare Rechner zur Verfügung gestellt, um sich den Anschein digitaler Weltläufigkeit zu geben. Sie hat diese Rechner wohl auch benutzt, um die Aktivitäten ihrer Schüler per *Remote Control* zu überwachen. Und auf diesem Wege möglicherweise sogar einen Blick in die Wohnzimmer ihrer Schüler erhascht. […]

Der zuständige Superintendent Christopher McGinley hat inzwischen auf seiner Webseite offiziell Stellung zu dem Fall genommen: Das Tracking-Feature auf den Schul-Laptops sei nur installiert worden, um gestohlene und verlorene Laptops wieder zu finden. Und das auch nur, wenn dafür eine schriftliche Zustimmung der Eltern vorlag. […]

Dass dies womöglich kein Einzelfall ist, belegt ein Ausschnitt aus der Sendung *Digital Nation* des Magazins *Frontline*. Auch darin kommt ein IT-Administrator einer Schule zu Wort, der in erstaunlicher Unbefangenheit davon berichtet, wie er die Rechner seiner Schüler kontrolliert. „Die merken gar nicht, dass sie beobachtet werden", sagt er darin. „Ich erlaube mir gerne einen kleinen Spaß mit ihnen und schieße ein Foto." […]

(283 Wörter)

Quelle: Tine Klopp, *Zeit online*, www.zeit.de, 19. Oktober, 2010.

a. Example:
The feature Remote Desktop can be used to monitor students at school. In this way teachers can not only check files saved on students' computers but they can also access students' web cameras and microphones.

b. ______________________________

c. ______________________________

d. ______________________________

e. ______________________________

c) **Analyze the main aspects of the cartoon by filling in the gaps.**

The cartoon shows a security checkpoint at a school bus [1] stop ________. Before students can [2.] ________ their school bus they must go through a [3.] ________. This looks like a security control at [4.] ________ In this way the [5.] ________ cannot only check students' [6.] ________ thoroughly but also their [7.] ________ for weapons and drugs. The authorities hope that the bus trip to school and lessons at school will be [8.] ________. Of course, the cartoonist [9.] ________ the issue but the cartoon shows a clear trend towards more safety [10.] ________ in and around schools.

d) **Analyze the following quotes.**

1. Find out if the quotes are for or against surveillance. Tick the appropriate box below each one.

A. **"The children are very happy here because they know they are on a school site where they are safe. They are in a position where they are not going to be robbed and harassed and so on."**
Quelle: Mike Rush, headteacher at a London high school, www.theguardian.com, August 4, 2009.

for ☐
against ☐

B. **"In some cases, teachers reported having their private conversations filmed when the school was not in session. […] No one should be subjected to the stress and pressure of being watched constantly."**
Quelle: Chris Keates, General Secretary at the National Association of Schoolmasters Union of Women Teachers, www.telegraph.co.uk, April 20, 2014.

for ☐
against ☐

C. **"If surveillance infiltrates our homes and personal relationships, that is a gross breach of our human and civil rights."**
Quelle: David Blunkett, British politician, www.theguardian.com, February 24, 2009.

for ☐
against ☐

2. Write down the main argument given in each quote in your own words.

Example:

Quote A: The first quote is in favour of security measures at schools. The headteacher says that the installation of cameras is accepted by the students in his school because they …

Quote B:

Quote C:

e) **Analyze the diagram "Safety and security measures" and explain the main facts in your own words. The prompts below the diagram can help you.**

Percentage of public schools that used selected safety and security measures, by year: School years 1999–2000, 2009–10, and 2013–14

Safety and security measures

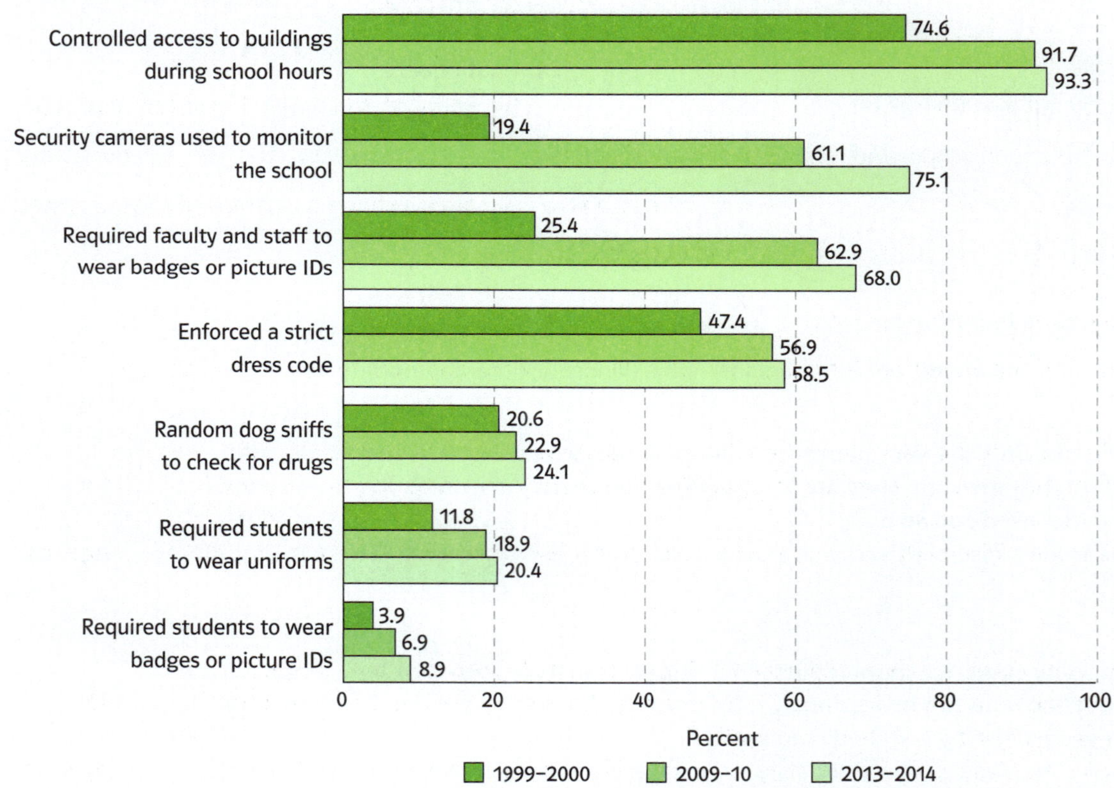

Quelle: Nach dem *National Centre for Education Statistics*, nces.ed.gov, May 2016.

General: bar chart – development of safety and security measures – development from 1999/2000 to 2013/14 – most commonly used measures – some measures not as widespread
Four most important measures: Controlled access …
Overall trend: sharp increase – slight rise
Conclusion: more and more safety and security measures – leads to the assumption that …

D | Practice

7 Political participation in the UK

► Vokabeln systematisch lernen, S. 238

Put the corresponding nouns in the boxes. Nouns which are in the same group use a common ending. Find these common endings and write them in the spaces under the boxes.

1.	discuss	
2.	decide	
3.	restrict	
4.	express	
5.	constitute	
6.	move	
7.	introduce	
8.	divide	
Common ending		

13.	examine	
14.	participate	
15.	publicize	
16.	present	
17.	discriminate	
18.	specify	
19.	motivate	
20.	declare	
Common ending		

9.	judge	
10.	develop	
11.	assign	
12.	argue	
Common ending		

21.	authorize	
22.	equalize	
23.	humanize	
24.	nationalize	
Common ending		

E | Reading +: The EU and refugees

8 Migrant boat disaster – Antonyms

→ page 136 ► Vokabeln systematisch lernen, S. 238

Find antonyms in the text for the words in the box below.

1.	closed	
2.	danger	
3.	births	
4.	emigration	
5.	harmless	
6.	confident	
7.	outside	
8.	sent	
9.	push	
10.	illegal	
11.	long-term	
12.	bright	

13.	hinder	
14.	unsystematic	
15.	private	
16.	unsafe	
17.	unlocked	
18.	exit	

Unit 11

Perspectives after college

A | Hörverstehen

1a Fragen zum Text

A 3.15

In der letzten Zeit ist in Großbritannien eine Diskussion über die berufliche Ausbildung entbrannt. Hören Sie einem Auszubildenden zu, der über seine Erfahrungen mit seiner beruflichen Ausbildung spricht, und beantworten Sie die folgenden Fragen in ganzen Sätzen auf Deutsch.

1. Was hatte Jack im Alter von siebzehn Jahren schon erreicht?

2. Warum entschied er sich gegen eine Fußballkarriere?

3. Was empfahl ihm sein Lehrer in der Schule?

4. In welchem Bereich suchte er eine Ausbildungsstelle?

5. Wo fing Jack seine Ausbildung an?

6. Was plant Jack nach seiner Ausbildung?

7. Warum ist er mit seinem jetzigen Leben zufrieden?

1b Satzergänzungen

A 3.16

Sie hören ein Interview mit Samantha, einer anderen Auszubildenden. Vervollständigen Sie die unten stehenden Sätze auf Deutsch mit Informationen aus dem Interview.

1. Samantha ging zur Arbeitsagentur, weil … ______________________

2. Sie fand ein Angebot für eine Ausbildungsstelle bei einer Firma, die … ______________________

3. Die Firma, bei der Samantha ihre Ausbildung absolviert, hat ihren Hauptsitz in Media City in Manchester, weil … ______________________

4. Samantha zog nach Manchester um, weil … ______________________

5. Sie muss das Berufskolleg in Manchester besuchen, da sie dort die Möglichkeit hat, … ______________________

6. Samantha hat bereits an einem interessanten Projekt mitgearbeitet, nämlich an … ______________________

B | Leseverstehen

2 Mediation

Unter Ihren Freunden wird diskutiert, wie man eine gute Bewerbung für eine Ausbildungsstelle schreibt. Sie haben den folgenden Zeitungsartikel gelesen und informieren Ihre Freunde über die wesentlichen Inhalte auf Deutsch.

School-leavers and graduates: how to write your first CV

[…] You've finished years of education and it's time to enter the world of work. The question you're undoubtedly facing now is: "How do I showcase years of education, achievements and outside interests on a CV?" There is no simple answer. Every CV is unique and needs to be tailored for each industry and company, so this is where your research needs to begin.

Recent research from the *National Citizen Service (NCS)* shows that employers have less and less time to review entry level CVs. On average you have just 8.8 seconds to stand out, so you need to be able to sell yourself and your strengths quickly.

First, study the company you're targeting. Have a look at their mission statement if it's online. Use any insight into the company and the role you're applying for to highlight how your skills and attributes would fit with the company you're applying to.

Numbers and percentages are always easy to digest quickly on a CV. If you can clearly show statistics that showcase your achievements then do so, but never exaggerate or embellish the truth. […]

You may think it can be difficult to stand out, but you just need to add [a] touch of personality. I always look for that something extra, something which shows your personal drive and ambition.

In an increasingly competitive job market, graduate recruits need to be able to demonstrate they have something more to offer than just academic performance. High grades don't guarantee a job or even an interview. The study by *NCS* goes on to reveal that half of employers would actually dismiss a CV if the candidate wasn't able to demonstrate experiences outside of the education system.

Highlight the work you have done outside school to show you're not afraid to put in the extra work for something you believe in. Academic qualifications are great to put on a CV and are incredibly important, but life experiences and extracurricular activities speak volumes about your character, not just your intelligence. An employer is looking for someone who can not only

get the job done, but someone who will fit within the culture of their organisation and get along with the team already in place. One example is to list any youth programmes you've participated in, any volunteering experiences, passion projects or sport and social activities that you actively pursue. […]

While you're writing your CV, keep asking yourself what you want this employer to know about you – what personal skills you are most proud of and how you could be an asset to their business. List specific skills that you have, such as confidence and resilience, presenting skills, the ability to work effectively in teams or examples of leading one. These traits are often neglected in CVs yet they are vital for the workplace. […]

You may have heard the advice that you should imitate your interviewer's movements and gestures as a technique to get them to trust you – the same can be said for CVs. Read the job description and copy the language they use. This will show that you not only read their brief fully, but you can use language that resonates with them. […]

Last but not least, we can often focus so much on making sure the content is right, that we forget the most obvious of rules. Your CV needs to look good as well as sound good. The top three things that turn off employers is bad grammar, spelling mistakes and poor formatting. Take advantage of simple online templates or even use your own creativity – just remember to have a fresh pair of eyes look at it before you send it out.

There's nothing to be afraid of when writing your first CV – it is ultimately all about you, and you know yourself best. If you get through to an interview my best advice is to be professional but more importantly be yourself. Enthusiasm and a keenness to learn are always attractive. Everyone knows a story about a person with the perfect grades that didn't get the job because they lacked personality, so make sure you bring that to the table too.

(699 words)

Quelle: Piers Linney, *The Guardian*, February 4, 2015, www.theguardian.com.

C | Textproduktion

3 Materialgestützter Aufsatz

Write a composition about the following topic.

- **Use the information of at least three of the given materials.**
- **Name which ones you are using.**
- **Make use of your own ideas.**
- **Do not write three separate compositions but one covering all the materials chosen.**

For some years now there has been a discussion about the possibilities that young people have after finishing school. Discuss the advantages and disadvantages of taking a gap year and state your point of view.

1

The big decision: should I take a gap year?

It may not be for everyone, but taking a year out can help you gain valuable experience – and even make you change course.

When I applied to university I thought seriously about taking a gap year. After a year at college, I was utterly demoralised. I hated the early mornings, and felt that I wouldn't have the motivation to attend university. I felt the best course of action would be to defer my application and have a year of saving up, hopefully gaining more work experience – and maybe even fit in some travelling. […]

In the end, I decided against taking a gap year – I wanted to study English literature, and thought a year out would mean my essay practice would diminish. I also knew that I could still keep my job at my local newspaper and my part-time job while I was there.

Weighing up all the options, a gap year no longer seemed relevant.

The idea of spending a year away from home is something that appeals to nearly everyone. So why is taking a gap year still considered the wildcard?

"We saw a presentation on taking gap years at college", says college student Holly Brooks. "But none of my friends fancied it, and I didn't want to

go it alone, especially considering the expense over the course of a year."

For a teenage student, the prospect of providing for yourself, miles away from home, can be daunting. This is the primary reason many give for not ticking the deferred entry option box and booking the round-the-world plane ticket. […]

Gap years aren't for everyone. Readjusting to an academic timetable after spending time abroad can be a shock. You also need to consider the practicalities, from financing your gap year to surviving without home comforts. […]

(306 words)

Quelle: Helen Whitehouse, *The Guardian*, June 27, 2013, www.theguardian.com.

Gap-Year-Programme

2

Das Gap-Year wird […] immer populärer und gehört in vielen angelsächsischen Ländern selbstverständlich in die Lebensplanung. […]

Sprachreisen
Sprachreisen können in Großstädte wie London oder New York führen, an die Strände von Barcelona, Miami oder Honolulu oder für den Arabischkurs in den Oman. Es gibt Kurse, bei denen die Unterkunft im Internat oder College angeboten wird. Man kann aber auch in einem Hotel, bei einer Gastfamilie oder in einer WG wohnen. Die Kosten variieren sehr stark, je nachdem, ob man eine Reise von zwei, drei Wochen oder drei Monaten plant oder gar ein Multi-Language-Year machen möchte. […]

„Work and Travel"
Als Au-pair in einer französischen Gastfamilie arbeiten oder in einem Hostel in Kanada aushelfen. So etwas lässt sich mit dem *„Work and Travel"*-Programm umsetzen. Altersbegrenzungen muss man bei den jeweiligen Botschaften erfragen.

Freiwilligendienste
Zum Angebot der *„Work and Travel"*-Agenturen zählen auch Freiwilligendienste. So kann man zum Beispiel eine Nichtregierungsorganisation in einem ghanaischen Dorf bei der HIV-Prävention unterstützen. […] Die Organisation *WWOOF (World-Wide Opportunities on Organic Farms)* vermittelt Aufenthalte auf Bauernhöfen in vielen Teilen der Welt. „Wwoofer" arbeiten gegen Kost und Logis auf den Höfen mit.

Berufserfahrung
Für ein Auslandspraktikum kann man deutsche, international aufgestellte Unternehmen fragen, ob eine Hospitanz in einer Auslandsvertretung möglich ist. Es gibt auch spezialisierte Agenturen, die Praktika vermitteln. […] Auch die Arbeitsagentur bietet in der Auslands- und Fachvermittlung Job- und Praktikums-möglichkeiten im Ausland an. Oder warum nicht Berufserfahrung als Ski-, Snowboard- oder Tauchlehrer sammeln?

(234 Wörter)

Quelle: Silke Weber, *Zeit Campus Ratgeber*, 26. September 2015, www.zeit.de.

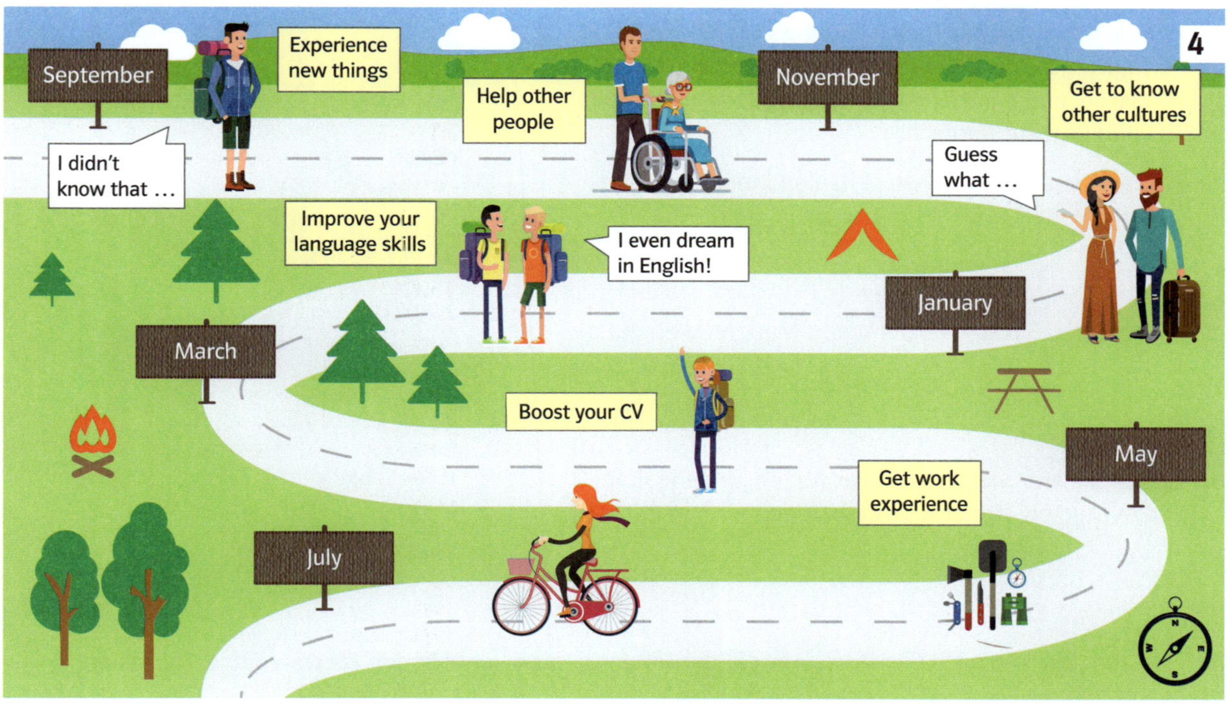

5

A. **"No one should undertake a gap year just to make their CV look good. In the end, you have to do what's right for you."**
Quelle: Stefan Wathan, chief executive of *Year Out Group*, www.telegraph.co.uk, July 18, 2015.

B. **"It's important to have goals to ensure a gap year's not just an extended holiday."**
Quelle: Dr Jennifer Wilby, senior lecturer and researcher at the *University of Hull Business School*, www.theguardian.com, August 26, 2015.

C. **"For pushing yourself out of your comfort zone, gap years are a must. You meet people with different lifestyles and from different cultures; it is about growing up and fending for yourself."**
Quelle: Jonathan Bryan, managing director of *Discover Adventure* in: *The Telegraph*, 29 July 2015.

D. **"One thing Africa is not short of is unskilled labour, so Western teenagers going over there to help can end up taking away jobs from local people."**
Quelle: Mark Watson, executive director of the charity *Tourism Concern*, www.theguardian.com, March 19, 2015.

Unit 12

Modern media and marketing

A | Hörverstehen

1a Fragen zum Text

A3.17

In der letzten Zeit ist die Diskussion über den Einfluss der Medien auf junge Menschen aufgeflammt. Hören Sie den Sprechern in der Radiosendung zu, die jeweils ihre Erfahrungen mit den Medien in Großbritannien präsentieren, und bearbeiten Sie die folgenden Aufgaben in Stichpunkten auf Deutsch.

1. Beschreiben Sie Christinas aktuellen Medienkonsum.

2. Beschreiben Sie auf welche Weise Mark Medien nutzt.

3. Zeigen Sie auf, wie in Christinas Augen junge Frauen in den Medien oft dargestellt werden.

4. Erläutern Sie, wie nach Christinas Ansicht der Umgang mit Alkohol in den Medien junge Menschen beeinflussen kann.

5. Erläutern Sie, welche Auswirkungen die zunehmend gewalttätigen Szenen in den Medien nach Marks Ansicht haben können.

6. Erläutern Sie, welche möglichen Lösungen Mark sieht.

1b Satzergänzungen

A3.18

Sie hören einen Ausschnitt aus einer Vorlesung an einer englischen Hochschule über die Auswirkungen von Massenmedien auf Kinder und Jugendliche. Ergänzen Sie die folgenden Sätze auf Deutsch.

1. Die Werbeindustrie spricht Jugendliche über die Medien an, weil … __________

2. Die Musikindustrie hat Jugendliche als Zielgruppe erkannt, weil … __________

3. Werbung in den Massenmedien kann einen negativen Einfluss auf Jugendliche ausüben, indem sie …

4. Eine Firma kann als positives Beispiel genannt werden, weil sie … __________

5. Regierungen können einen positiven Beitrag leisten, wenn sie … __________

B | Leseverstehen

2 Mediation

Unter Ihren Freunden ist eine Diskussion über die möglichen Gefahren der sozialen Medien entbrannt. Sie haben den folgenden Artikel gelesen und informieren Ihre Freunde anhand des Zeitungsartikels über die Auswirkungen von sozialen Medien auf Jugendliche.

Teens' night-time use of social media 'risks harming mental health'

Teenagers who engage with social media during the night could be damaging their sleep and increasing their risk of depression and anxiety, research shows.

More than 460 teenagers at a secondary school in Scotland were questioned about their general social media habits, and in particular their night-time use of sites such as *Facebook* and *Twitter*, as part of the study by Glasgow University.

It found that while overall use of social media affects the quality of sleep, those who log on at night to respond to alerts are particularly affected. It remains unclear, however, whether it is social media that is damaging sleep, or whether teenagers turn to social media because they can't sleep for some other reason.

Dr Heather Cleland Woods said her study had found that children as young as 11 were on *Facebook* and *Twitter* and using them considerably. Some pupils at the Glasgow school were using multiple devices – a phone and a tablet for example – to view multiple sites simultaneously and were on them "into the early hours of the morning".

Cleland Woods, who presented the paper at a *British Psychological Society* conference in Manchester on Friday, said: "Adolescence can be a period of increased vulnerability for the onset of depression and anxiety, and poor sleep quality may contribute to this."

"It is important that we understand how social media use relates to these. Evidence is increasingly supporting a link between social media use and wellbeing, particularly during adolescence, but the causes of this are unclear."

She continued: "While overall social media use impacts on sleep quality, those who log on at night appear to be particularly affected. This may be mostly true of individuals who are highly emotionally invested. This means we have to think about how our kids use social media, in relation to time for switching off."

Cleland Woods, a mother of two whose background is in sleep research, posed the idea of a "digital sunset": in the same way that the sun sets a couple of hours before bed, we do the same with our digital devices before bedtime to potentially improve sleep.

As well as being asked about their social media habits, the pupils, aged between 11 and 17, were also asked to respond to a questionnaire which measured sleep quality, self-esteem, anxiety and depression. They were also asked about their emotional investment in social media, the pressure they felt to be available 24/7, and the resulting anxiety if they did not respond immediately to texts or posts.

Preliminary analysis of the research showed overall social media use, and specifically night-time use, was related to poorer sleep quality, lower self-esteem and higher levels of anxiety and depression. A pronounced emotional investment in social media had a similar effect.

Separately, a study of teenage stress commissioned by the *National Citizen's Service* youth programme suggests that girls seek comfort from social media when they are anxious and worried.

The survey of 1,000 12–18-year-olds found that nine out of 10 teenage girls have experienced stress in the past year, with seven in 10 cases leading to symptoms of stress-related illnesses.

Rather than talking to their parents, girls are more likely to turn to social media, distracting themselves from the pressure they're under by Snapchatting friends or browsing *Facebook*.

The survey suggests that girls are likely to experience stress more frequently than boys, and more often than the average adult, with girls feeling stressed an average of twice a week.

The cause of stress, the survey suggests, is increasingly the anxiety of making important life decisions, with many teenagers suffering from decision paralysis. It found the top three sources of stress for girls were exam results (57 %), making decisions about the future (37 %) and arguments with friends (36 %).

Lucie Russell, campaigns director at the youth mental health charity *Young Minds*, said: "We should not underestimate the huge amount of pressure young people are facing, especially at this time of year which brings the uncertainties that come with a new academic year.

"Not only has social media added new complexities to their daily lives, but looming, uncertain futures just add to this stress. We need to ensure young people are equipped with the skills to deal with these pressures and to navigate positive paths into adulthood."

(720 words)

Quelle: Sally Weale, *The Guardian*, September 11, 2015, www.theguardian.com.

C | Textproduktion

3 Materialgestützter Aufsatz

Write a composition about the following topic.
- **Use the information of at least three of the given materials.**
- **Name which ones you are using.**
- **Make use of your own ideas.**
- **Do not write three separate compositions but one covering all the materials chosen.**

For some years now there has been a discussion about the effects of advertising on young people. Discuss the statement "Alcohol advertising should be banned or restricted on TV and the Internet".

Facebook deal with Diageo fuels under-age drinking fears 1

Drinks giant's marketing tie-up on advertising pages raises concerns about health impact on teenagers.

A multimillion-dollar deal agreed between *Facebook* and drinks company *Diageo* will fuel the under-age drinking epidemic by exposing increasing numbers of young people to alcohol marketing, health experts are warning.

[...] Health experts and alcohol campaigners say the impact will be felt in teenage drinking. Dr Nick Sheron, a liver specialist at Southampton hospital, is one of those who believes the attraction of *Facebook* is the youth of its users, with half under the age of 24 and many under the legal drinking age of 18.

Facebook argues that pages set up by alcohol advertisers are "age-gated", and therefore only accessible to those who are over 18. But Sheron argues that many younger people do not disclose their true age on *Facebook*.

"The age verification process for social networking sites is clearly completely ineffective –

even though users are supposed to be 13 or above, it has been suggested that one-quarter of UK children aged 8–12 have a *Facebook* or similar account," he said

"Secondly, the majority of these accounts are hidden from parents, so *Diageo* effectively has a private narrowcast channel of communication with young people, which it will use to promote alcohol use as a positive lifestyle." [...]

Facebook said it was very hard to control the age group who access any internet site, but insisted that it does all it can. [...]

"It shouldn't be forgotten that making sure services are age-appropriate isn't an issue that is confined to *Facebook* – teens and young people use the wider internet every day, often accessing websites and online services that offer few or no safety tools. We feel that the best solution to using services in an age-appropriate way is for service providers like *Facebook* to carry on working with parents, safety experts and kids themselves to aid education and understanding."

(322 words)

Quelle: Sarah Boseley, *The Guardian*, September 20, 2011.

2

TV-Werbung für Alkohol verführt Jugendliche

[...] Alkoholwerbung im Fernsehen verführt Kinder und Jugendliche nach einer Studie von Kieler Wissenschaftlern zum Rauschtrinken. Das häufige Sehen von TV-Werbespots erhöhe das Risiko des sogenannten Komasaufens bis zu viermal. [...]

Bei den Befragten, die am wenigsten Werbung mit Alkohol sahen, hatten der Studie zufolge 6,2 Prozent mehr als fünf Rauscherlebnisse in dem Befragungszeitraum. Bei den Teilnehmern, die am häufigsten TV-Spots für Bier, Wein und Schnaps gesehen hatten, lag die Rauschquote bei 24 Prozent und damit viermal so hoch.

Die Langzeituntersuchung bestätigt nach Angabe der *DAK-Gesundheit* zudem, dass ein riskanter Alkoholkonsum ein verbreitetes Phänomen in Deutschland ist. Die Hälfte der teilnehmenden Schüler habe über ein erstmaliges Rauschtrinken – das sind mindestens fünf alkoholische Getränke bei einer Gelegenheit – innerhalb von 30 Monaten berichtet. 11 Prozent der Mädchen und 18 Prozent der Jungen gaben an, sie hätten sogar mehr als fünf Erfahrungen mit derartig massivem Alkoholkonsum. [...]

„Unsere Studie zeigt, dass Alkoholwerbung von Jugendlichen nicht nur wahrgenommen wird", erklärte der Suchtexperte der *DAK-Gesundheit*, Ralf Kremer. „Die Werbung kann vielmehr als unabhängiger Risikofaktor für die Initiierung des häufigen Rauschtrinkens im Jugendalter angesehen werden." Die Krankenkasse und das *IFT-Nord*, die seit sechs Jahren auch eine gemeinsame Anti-Alkohol-Kampagne betreiben, plädierten für Werbeverbote und die Erziehung der Kinder zu einem kritischen Umgang mit den Werbespots.

(215 Wörter)

Quelle: *N-TV*, 06. Oktober 2015, www.n-tv.de.

3

4

A. **"The alcohol industry is sidestepping advertising rules by targeting young people, implying that drinking will bring friends and fun."**
Quelle: Sarah Boseley, health expert, *The Guardian*, www.theguardian.com, January 21, 2010.

B. **"Underage drinking is declining in this country, where we have alcohol advertising, and in France it is going up, where they've banned it."**
Quelle: Ian Twinn, *ISBA, The Voice of British Advertisers* Director of Public Affairs, www.bbc.com, June 12, 2013.

C. **"Children and young people are seeing more alcohol advertising than in the past and are better able to recognise alcohol brands than those of cakes or ice cream."**
Quelle: Eric Appleby, *Alcohol Concern* chief executive, www.bbc.com, June 12, 2013.

5

Long-term effects of alcohol

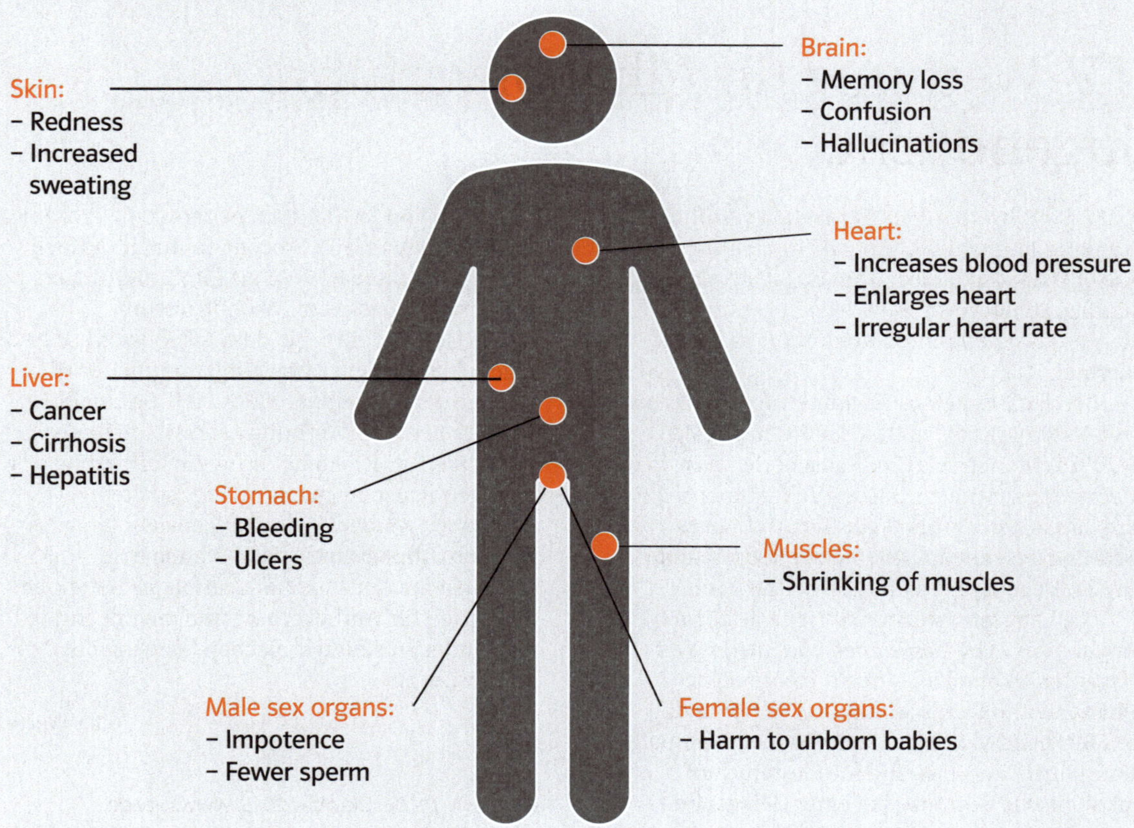

Unit 13

Social problems: How to deal with money

A | Hörverstehen

1a Offene Fragen

A 3.19

In der letzten Zeit wird viel über die zunehmenden Schuldenprobleme von Jugendlichen und Studierenden diskutiert. Hören Sie das Interview im englischen Radio, in dem zwei Studenten und ein Schuldnerberater von ihren Erfahrungen berichten. Beantworten Sie die folgenden Fragen in Stichpunkten auf Deutsch.

1. Warum können die beiden Studenten ihren Lebensunterhalt nicht mehr wie bisher finanzieren?

2. Welche Art Sommerurlaub konnten Debbie und Kieran sich noch im letzten Jahr leisten?

3. Welche finanziellen Probleme haben sich für die Studenten nach ihrer Urlaubsreise ergeben?

4. Mit welchen finanziellen Problemen sehen sich Studenten laut dem Schuldnerberater nach dem Studium konfrontiert?

5. Welche zwei Listen sollen Debbie und Kieran auf Anraten des Schuldnerberaters aufstellen?

1b Satzergänzungen

A 3.20

Die neuesten Statistiken zur Kinderarmut zeigen, dass 27 Prozent (3,6 Millionen) der Kinder im Vereinigten Königreich in Armut leben. Die Radiosprecherin Jessie Sanders hat Mary Wintour von der Stadtverwaltung in Manchester eingeladen, um mit ihr über Kinderarmut zu sprechen. Hören Sie das Interview und vervollständigen Sie die unten stehenden Sätze auf Deutsch.

1. Relative Armut im Vereinigten Königreich bedeutet, dass … ______

2. Zu den Grundbedürfnissen der Menschen gehören laut Mary Wintour … ______

3. Mary ist der Meinung, dass es neben der Erfüllung der Grundbedürfnisse für Kinder ebenfalls wichtig ist, … ______

4. Als Gründe für Kinderarmut nennt Mary … ______

5. Laut Mary ist es für Kinder aus armen Familien weniger wahrscheinlich, dass sie … ______

6. Laut Mary ist es wahrscheinlicher, dass Kinder aus armen Familien … ______

7. Als Maßnahmen der Regierung, Kinderarmut zu bekämpfen, nennt Mary … ______

B | Leseverstehen

2 Mediation

Unter Ihren Freunden ist eine Diskussion darüber entstanden, wie hoch die Kosten für Ihre Abschlussfeier an der Schule sein dürfen. Sie haben den folgenden Zeitungsartikel über eine Studie der Kreditkartenfirma Visa gelesen, in dem es um die Kosten von Schulabschlussfeiern in den USA geht. Informieren Sie Ihre Klassenkameraden anhand des Artikels darüber, wie teuer solche Feiern in den USA sind und wofür die Schüler das Geld ausgeben.

Prom night can cost teenagers (and parents) a pretty penny

On average, US families are spending as much as $ 919 on their teen's prom expenses

Prom, for Brianna Albert, was an experience she will never forget – and not just because two of her classmates got into a fight over wearing the same dress. While she has fond memories of last year's "night to remember", she remembers the cost and the stress too.

Many US teenagers and parents are feeling those same stresses now as prom season gets into full swing again. A recent survey from *Visa* showed that the average US family plans to spend about $ 919 on a prom-going teen, with parents covering as much as 73 % of the costs. [...]

Albert said that her parents – a preschool teacher and a lawyer – paid for the dress, her hair and her share of the costs of a limo rental. "My dress was relatively inexpensive. Luckily, it was only $ 80. I actually didn't even find my dress [...]," she said, explaining that her mom bought it while on a trip to Boston. [...]

With this year's proms just weeks away, teenagers at high schools across the US are already racking up hundreds of dollars in prom-related expenses. [...]

Families with lower incomes spend the most, according to the *Visa* survey. Families with income below $ 25,000 planned to spend $ 1,393 while families with income below $ 50,000 planned to spend $ 1,109 and families with income over $ 50,000 planned to spend an average of $ 799.

"I can't really imagine spending $ 1,000 on prom myself," said Morgan [high school student]. "If someone did, they might [hire] a limo, professional photographer with professional lighting – apparently that's a thing – and buy a really fancy dress, expensive flowers like orchids, fancy dinner, etc."

There are others, however, who could easily find a way to spend a $ 1,000. "I can definitely see myself spending $ 1,000 on prom. Last year, since I went to two proms, I spent around $ 900," Esther Galo, 18, told the *Guardian*. [...]

Galo said that her mom, who works as a nurse, paid for all of her prom expenses. To get the best deal on items like makeup, tanning and limo, they looked to Groupon or Living Social for discounts. [...]

Promposals

It's not just the girls who begin planning and spending money months beforehand.

"It's no longer acceptable to just 'ask' a girl to prom," Ashleigh Prendable, a teacher at Albert's school, the Colonel Zadok Magruder high school in Gaithersburg, Maryland, told the *Guardian*.

As a result, promposals – elaborate invitations to proms – are setting some US teenagers back by as much as $ 324, according to *Visa's* survey.

Prendable's students have devised scavenger hunts, flashmobs, and even built their prom proposals into lesson plans. One student got a math teacher to devise a problem with the variables P, R and M – instead of the usual X, Y and Z – and the number 0. [...]

No teen left behind

To make sure that underprivileged students are not left out of the end-of-the-year activities, nonprofits like *Operation Prom* and *Cinderella* and *Prince Charming Project* are providing low-income students with free formal wear.

"Senior year is a tough year," Noel D'Allacco, founder of *Operation Prom*, told *CNN*. "You already have to think about the costs for college so then tacking on the price tag of the dress, the tuxedo rental, the prom tickets, the limo, the flowers, the hair, the makeup, everything that you need, you are looking at a lot of money that families and the students are worried about that senior year." [...]

While the teens are excited for their upcoming proms, they insist that the night is "really not a huge deal".

"It's weird because it's expected to be this huge thing, so you spend all this money on it, but many at my school would agree that it's not the end-all-be-all that it once was," said Morgan. [...]

Galo, on the other hand, believes that spending money on prom is a worthy investment.

"For me, since prom only happens twice in your life, it is worth investing in it. You want to look back on pictures and remember the fun you had and how it was a night you felt and looked your best," she said. "The memories you make will last forever, so you want to make sure they're good ones!"

(726 words)

Quelle: Jana Kasperkevic, *The Guardian*, April 20, 2015, www.theguardian.com.

C | Textproduktion

3 Materialgestützter Aufsatz

Write a composition about the following topic.
- **Use the information of at least three of the given materials.**
- **Name which ones you are using.**
- **Make use of your own ideas.**
- **Do not write three separate compositions but one covering all the materials chosen.**

For some years now there has been a discussion about the effect of money on international sport. Discuss the influence of money on sports and state your point of view.

1

Female sport stars should earn the same as their male counterparts

[...] I remember picking up my first winner's cheque of €500 at a small competition in Ireland and thinking I had made it. Until I realised that men in the 100m at the same event received €2,000. It was a rude awakening.

Although many sports have moved into the 21st century and award equal prize money at major competitions, 30% of sports, including football, cricket and squash, refuse to move forward, as was highlighted this week in a study by the *BBC*. [...]

It has been argued that women's sport isn't as businesslike as men's, that it doesn't generate enough interest to justify equality on the pay scale. But this is because they refuse to give women's sport the same platform. Many of the sports that offer equal pay also allow both men and women the chance to share a platform: athletics, cycling, skating and swimming have world championships that both genders are able to participate in. [...]

I was always cautious when discussing how much money I would make from sport, especially surrounding sponsorship contracts. I had seen proof that I wasn't getting the best deal and suspected that it wasn't based on performance, but rather my gender. Young male sprinters would receive more media attention and more money, having not achieved the levels I had reached. [...]

It wasn't until three substandard kit contracts later in my career that I realised just because you are living your dream, it doesn't mean you can't want more from it financially.

(260 words)

Quelle: Jeanette Kwakye, *The Guardian*, October 31, 2014, www.theguardian.com.

2

Her mit dem Geld!

[…] Eine Viertelmilliarde US-Dollar ist eine Menge Geld. Vor allem, wenn man es dafür erhält, ein kleines Logo auf dem Hemd zu tragen und den Golfschläger zu wechseln. Umgerechnet knapp 200 Millionen Euro soll der Sportartikelhersteller *Nike* dem Golfer Rory McIlroy bieten, damit er die nächsten zehn Jahre das Häkchenlogo spazieren trägt. Wird der von amerikanischen Medien vermeldete Deal offiziell bestätigt, dann stellt der 23-jährige Nordire einen neuen Sponsoringrekord im Sport auf. […]

Der neue Rekord lässt Fragen über den Sinn und Unsinn des Sponsorings von Sportlern aufkommen. Seit Anbeginn des Profitums unter Athleten gang und gäbe, investieren Unternehmen Unsummen nicht nur in Klubs und Mannschaften, deren Fortbestand, Popularität und teils auch Erfolg zumindest annähernd sicher ist, sondern auch in Sportler, deren Karriere jeden Moment vorbei sein könnte.

Dem Risiko zum Trotz, sagt Pascal Schulte vom Branchen-Analysten „Sport+Markt“. „Der Vertrag macht aus Sicht von *Nike* durchaus Sinn. Golf ist vor allem in den englischsprachigen Ländern sehr beliebt, dort wird es sogar in Kneipen übertragen.“ Vor allem der US-Riese *Nike* ist immer wieder für rekordverdächtige Sponsorendeals gut, denn sie haben den Konzern zur Weltmarke gemacht. […]

Mancher Profi veränderte für einen Sponsorenvertrag sogar sein Äußeres. Paul Breitner, wegen seiner Afrofrisur und seinem nicht gerade latent zur Schau gestellten Interesse am Kommunismus als „Revoluzzer“ betitelt, trug viele Jahre einen prächtigen Vollbart. Kurz vor der Fußball-Weltmeisterschaft 1982 schor der Nationalspieler den Bart ab und warb für einen Rasierwasser-Hersteller, dem dieser Coup 150.000 Mark wert war.

Zuweilen werben Sportler auch für Dinge, mit denen sie sich weniger identifizieren konnten oder nach eigener Aussage keine Verwendung dafür hatten. Pelé, Brasiliens Fußball-Idol, warb vor einigen Jahren für die Potenzpille *Viagra*, wurde aber nicht müde zu betonen, das Produkt nie genommen zu haben. […]

Nach den guten Erfahrungen mit Tiger Woods will *Nike* McIlroy als neues Gesicht der Marke aufbauen. „Für einen 23-Jährigen ist McIlroy schon sehr weit, er kann der Golf-Superstar der nächsten Jahre werden“, sagt Schulte. Denn Woods’ Image hat trotz des sportlich erfolgreichen Comebacks Schaden genommen durch private Eskapaden. Von Lance Armstrong trennte sich das Unternehmen wegen dessen Dopingskandal. […]

(344 Wörter)

Quelle: Dominik Bardow und Sebastian Stier, *Der Tagesspiegel*, 10. Januar 2013, www.tagesspiegel.de.

3

4

A. **“When money comes in at the door, sport flies out the window.”**
Quelle: H.A. Harris, *Sport in Greece and Rome*, p. 40, Cornell University Press, 1972.

B. **“An athlete cannot run with money in his pockets. He must run with hope in his heart and dreams in his head.”**
Quelle: Emil Zatopek, Czech Republic Olympic athletics champion, 1952.

C. **“It’s obvious that children growing up idolising sporting heroes with beer brands blazoned across their chests will develop deep-rooted positive attitudes towards drinking.”**
Quelle: Katherine Brown, director of the *British Institute of Alcohol Studies, The Guardian*, www.theguardian.com, December 25, 2014.

5

Highest-Paying Sports Leagues – Average Player Salaries (2014 – 15) [in millions of $US dollars]

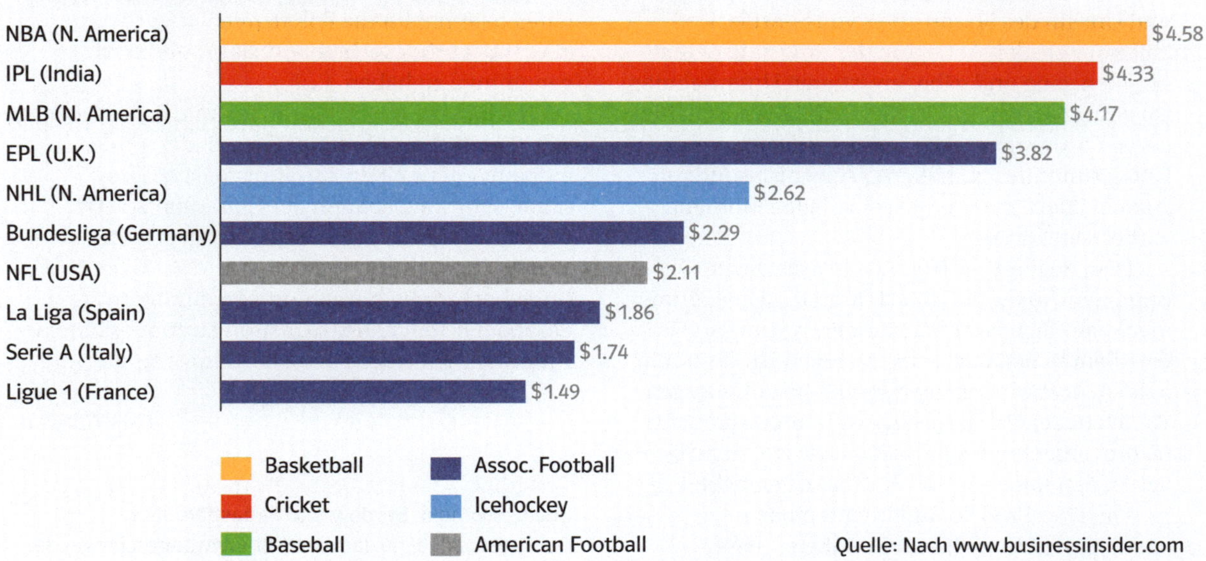

Quelle: Nach www.businessinsider.com

Unit 14

Technological developments and environment

A | Hörverstehen

1a Offene Fragen

A 3.21

Seit dem Jahr 2013 findet alle zwei Jahre die Europäische Konferenz zur Klimaanpassung statt, um über technologische Entwicklungen zu beraten, die helfen können, den Klimawandel aufzuhalten. Hören Sie den Sprechern zu, die jeweils über die Forschungstätigkeiten in ihren Firmen berichten, und bearbeiten Sie die folgenden Fragen auf Deutsch.

1. Welche technische Neuerung wird in der Firma *Severn Soft Cells* gegenwärtig entwickelt?

2. Wie funktioniert das Produkt der Firma *Severn Soft Cells*?

3. Welche Vorteile wird das Produkt der Firma *Severn Soft Cells* in der Zukunft haben?

4. Was geschieht laut John Skinner von der Firma *RecycleMore* mit herkömmlichen Batterien, wenn sie leer sind?

5. Wie unterscheidet sich das Produkt der Firma *RecycleMore* von herkömmlichen Produkten, die bereits auf dem Markt sind?

1b Satzergänzungen

A 3.22

In einer Radiosendung sprechen die Gäste über den Faktor „Stress“, den sie in einer Großstadt wie London erleben. Hören Sie den Sprechern zu und vervollständigen die unten stehenden Sätze auf Deutsch.

1. Für Indira Khan ist die Luftverschmutzung in London der schlimmste Stressfaktor, da sie … ____________________
2. Zudem findet Indira, das anonyme Leben in Großstädten führe dazu, dass die Menschen … ____________________
3. Laut Tony Green wird das Stressniveau in großen Städten erhöht durch … ____________________
4. Wenn Indira jeden Morgen von Nord-London in die Innenstadt fährt, steigt sie erst in … ____________________ und dann … ____________________
5. Tonys Stressniveau ist gestiegen, seitdem … ____________________
6. Tonys Arzt hat ihm empfohlen, … ____________________

B | Leseverstehen

2 Mediation

Unter Ihren Freunden ist eine Diskussion aufgekommen über die Auswirkungen moderner Technologie auf unsere Gesundheit. Sie haben den folgenden Artikel gelesen, in dem es um die Auswirkungen moderner Medien auf unser Gehirn geht. Informieren Sie Ihre Freunde anhand des Zeitungsartikels.

Why the modern world is bad for your brain

[…] Our brains are busier than ever before. We're assaulted with facts, pseudo facts, jibber-jabber, and rumour, all posing as information. Trying to figure out what you need to know and what you can ignore is exhausting. At the same time, we are all doing more. Thirty years ago, travel agents made our airline and rail reservations, salespeople helped us find what we were looking for in shops, and professional typists or secretaries helped busy people with their correspondence. Now we do most of those things ourselves. We are doing the jobs of 10 different people while still trying to keep up with our lives, our children and parents, our friends, our careers, our hobbies, and our favourite TV shows.

Our smartphones have become Swiss army knife-like appliances that include a dictionary, calculator, web browser, email, *Game Boy*,

appointment calendar, voice recorder, guitar tuner, weather forecaster, GPS, texter, tweeter, *Facebook* updater, and flashlight. They're more powerful and do more things than the most advanced computer at *IBM* corporate head-quarters 30 years ago. And we use them all the time, part of a 21st-century mania for cramming everything we do into every single spare moment of downtime. We text while we're walking across the street, catch up on email while standing in a queue – and while having lunch with friends, we surreptitiously check to see what our other friends are doing. [...]

But there's a fly in the ointment. Although we think we're doing several things at once, multitasking, this is a powerful and diabolical illusion. Earl Miller, a neuroscientist at *MIT* and one of the world experts on divided attention, says that our brains are "not wired to multitask well... When people think they're multitasking, they're actually just switching from one task to another very rapidly. And every time they do, there's a cognitive cost in doing so." [...] Even though we think we're getting a lot done, ironically, multitasking makes us demonstrably less efficient. Multitasking has been found to increase the production of the stress hormone cortisol as well as the fight-or-flight hormone adrenaline, which can overstimulate your brain and cause mental fog or scrambled thinking. [...]

In the old days, if the phone rang and we were busy, we either didn't answer or we turned the ringer off. When all phones were wired to a wall, there was no expectation of being able to reach us at all times – one might have gone out for a walk or been between places – and so if someone couldn't reach you (or you didn't feel like being reached), it was considered normal. Now more people have mobile phones than have toilets. This has created an implicit expectation that you should be able to reach someone when it is convenient for you, regardless of whether it is convenient for them. [...]

Glenn Wilson, former visiting professor of psychology at Gresham College, London, calls it infomania. His research found that being in a situation where you are trying to concentrate on a task, and an email is sitting unread in your inbox, can reduce your effective IQ by 10 points. [...]

Russ Poldrack, a neuroscientist at Stanford, found that learning information while multitasking causes the new information to go to the wrong part of the brain. If students study and watch TV at the same time, for example, the information from their schoolwork goes into the striatum, a region specialised for storing new procedures and skills, not facts and ideas. Without the distraction of TV, the information goes into the hippocampus, where it is organised and categorised in a variety of ways, making it easier to retrieve. [...]

In discussing information overload with *Fortune 500* leaders, top scientists, writers, students, and small business owners, email comes up again and again as a problem. It's not a philosophical objection to email itself, it's the mind-numbing number of emails that come in. When the 10-year-old son of my neuroscience colleague Jeff Mogil (head of the Pain Genetics lab at McGill University) was asked what his father does for a living, he responded, "He answers emails." Jeff admitted after some thought that it's not so far from the truth. [...]

Before email, if you wanted to write to someone, you had to invest some effort in it. You'd sit down with pen and paper, or at a typewriter, and carefully compose a message. [...] Because the very act of writing a note or letter to someone took this many steps, and was spread out over time, we didn't go to the trouble unless we had something important to say. Because of email's immediacy, most of us give little thought to typing up any little thing that pops in our heads and hitting the send button. [...]

(798 words)

Quelle: Daniel J Levitin, *The Guardian*, January 18, 2015, www.theguardian.com.

C | Textproduktion

3 Materialgestützter Aufsatz

Write a composition about the following topic.

- **Use the information of at least three of the given materials.**
- **Name which ones you are using.**
- **Make use of your own ideas.**
- **Do not write three separate compositions but one covering all the materials chosen.**

For some years now there has been a discussion about the possibility of banning cars in inner cities. Discuss the pros and cons of this suggestion and state your point of view.

1

How to create healthier cities

Air quality is deteriorating in many of the world's cities. Nearly two-thirds of people with diabetes live in urban areas. Wealthier lifestyles, prioritising convenience and fast food, have led even formerly famine-stricken China to admit an obesity epidemic. Urban dwellers have far-higher stress levels than their rural counterparts.

If that's city living, who'd do it?

Well, 54 % of us and counting. With that much of the world's population living in urban areas, cities surely have a duty to do a better job of protecting public health. It's not only a question of residents' wellbeing: cities with physically active residents are more economically productive than their sedentary counterparts.

Many cities have started to take health seriously. Copenhagen replaced a driving culture with one of walking and cycling. Sydney is stocked with high quality sports clubs and facilities. Singapore's expert grasp of data and technology has led to low-carbon and sustainable models of urban design.

Even Tokyo, the world's biggest city, has one of the world's best public transport systems meaning it keeps greenhouse gas emissions relatively low. And Hong Kong may have an extremely dense population, but its residents often travel on foot and many of them are doctors.

(203 words)

Quelle: Tamsin Rutter, *The Guardian*, October 12, 2015, www.theguardian.com.

2

„Autofreie Städte? Wunderbar!"

„Sicher müssen Autos raus aus der Stadt. Ich habe seit 33 Jahren keins mehr", schreibt der Grünen-Abgeordnete Michael Cramer in der aktuellen Wochenendausgabe der *taz*. Cramer sitzt für die Grünen im Europaparlament und weist darauf hin, dass seine Partei schon 1984 die Idee der autofreien Städte propagiert habe.

„Die Große Koalition wollte daraufhin den Autoanteil auf 20 Prozent senken." Und heute? Führe die autofixierte Stadtentwicklungspolitik ins Chaos. Bus und Bahn seien zu teuer, die Parkgebühren dafür zu billig. [...]

Für die Sicherheit der Bürger wäre eine Einschränkung des Verkehrs wohl besser. Mehr als 3.500 Menschen sterben jährlich in Deutschland im Straßenverkehr, insgesamt gab es im Jahr 2010 knapp 2,5 Millionen Unfälle mit motorisierten Fahrzeugen, die volkswirtschaftlichen Kosten betragen laut der Bundesanstalt für Straßenwesen 31 Milliarden Euro.

Also Kraftfahrzeuge verbannen – und alles wird gut? Nein, schreibt die Rennfahrerin Ellen Lohr. Allerdings nicht, weil sie mit ihrem *Lamborghini* unbedingt durch die Stadt rasen will. „Ich habe drei Kinder", sagt sie. „Jeden, der von einer autofreien Stadt träumt, würde ich gern mit dem *Maxi Cosi* in der Hand zum Kinderarzt schicken, während zwei andere Kids rumnerven." Lohr hofft, dass die Zukunft uns eben nicht Ideen wie in London oder Turin beschert, wo die Innenstadt beispielsweise Maut kostet.

Die österreichische Köchin und überzeugte Fußgängerin Sarah Wiener sieht das ganz anders. Sie schreibt: „Autofreie Städte! Wunderbar!" Wiener glaubt, die Menschen würden so automatisch gesünder, agiler und bewegungsfreudiger. In Italien und Südfrankreich gebe es doch schon autofreie Dörfer und Kleinstädte. Die Erfahrung dort – wie auch in autofreien Stadtteilen in Münster oder Freiburg: Die Lebensqualität steige schlagartig. [...]

Die Fahrradkurierin Anja Rillcke aus Köln hält eine autofreie Stadt für keine so gute Idee. Dann wäre doch der alltägliche Machtkampf – Auto gegen Rad – vorbei.

(289 Wörter)

Quelle: Emilia Smechowski, *TAZ*, 24.03.2012, www.taz.de.

3

"Isn't it nice to see children cycling to school?"

4

A. **"Electric vehicles offer a real advantage in reducing the dangerous nitrogen oxide and particulate matter in urban areas."**
Quelle: Ian Walker / Gustav Bösehans, www.theguardian.com, January 8, 2016.

B. **"Carpooling is important for urban density, air pollution and other reasons."**
Quelle: Clay Shirky, American writer and teacher, www.wired.com, August 20, 2008.

C. **"Whereas a personally owned car caters for an individual or a family, a car-club car can service 60 people. [...]. Private cars are wasteful and expensive."**
Quelle: Stephen Moss, www.theguardian.com, April 28, 2015.

5

a) Attitudes to electric cars and vans in 2015

Question: Which of these statements best describes your current attitude towards buying an electric car or van?

	2015
I already own an electric car or van	0%
I am thinking about buying an electric car or van quite soon	1%
I am thinking about buying an electric car or van, but I haven't thought about when I will buy it	4%
I thought about buying one, but decided not to at this stage	16%
I haven't really thought about buying an electric car or van	56%
I have never heard of electric cars or vans	1%
I don't drive / don't need a car	14%
I don't know	6%
No response	2%

b) Factors deterring people from buying an electric car or van in 2015

Question: If you were to buy a car or van in the next 12 months, what, if anything, would put you off buying an electric car or van? (Full driving licence holders only [...])

	2015
Limited choice (not many vehicles to choose from)	6%
Lack of knowledge	13%
Cost	27%
Battery: distance travelled on charge	36%
Recharging	39% [...]
The vehicle: performance, size / practicality, looks	8%
Technology: doesn't work / not proven	8% [...]
Don't know	7%

More than one response allowed [...]
Quelle: Nach 2015 & 2014 Office for National Statistics Omnibus/Opinion Survey, Tables ATT0503 und ATT0506, 18 June 2015.

Unit 15

Going global

A | Hörverstehen

1a Offene Fragen

A 3.23

In der letzten Zeit ist eine Diskussion über die Auswirkungen des Massentourismus aufgekommen. Hören Sie den zwei Experten auf dem Gebiet des internationalen Tourismus zu und beantworten Sie die folgenden Fragen in Stichpunkten auf Deutsch.

1. Wie viele Touristen werden laut Oliver Parkin in den nächsten 15 Jahren verreisen?

2. Welche zwei negativen Auswirkungen des Massentourismus nennt Oliver Parkin?

3. Wie hat Manee Luang zu nachhaltigem Tourismus beigetragen?

4. Wie erfolgreich ist Manee Luang?

5. Wie nachhaltig ist der Massentourismus heute laut Oliver Parkin?

1b Satzergänzungen

A 3.24

Sie hören den Ausschnitt aus einem Vortrag eines Mitarbeiters einer Menschenrechtsorganisation. Er spricht über die Möglichkeiten internationaler Hotelketten, Kinderausbeutung weltweit zu bekämpfen. Ergänzen Sie die folgenden Sätze auf Deutsch

1. Die Tourismusindustrie ist in den letzten Jahren stark gewachsen, weil wir in den westlichen Ländern …

2. Der Massentourismus bringt negative Begleiterscheinungen mit sich, weil ...

3. Wenn junge Menschen Arbeitsplätze in Urlaubsorten in Entwicklungsländern bekommen, müssen sie oft ...

4. Der zusätzliche Einsatz von Lernprogrammen vermittelt den Hotelangestellten die Fähigkeit, ...

5. In nicht wenigen Ländern werden Kinder eingesetzt, um ...

B | Leseverstehen

2 Mediation

Die Herstellung modischer Kleidung zu günstigen Preisen ist ein globales Problem und hat spätestens seit der Katastrophe in einer Textilfabrik in Bangladesch die Aufmerksamkeit westlicher Staaten auf sich gelenkt. Für Ihre Schülerzeitung möchten Sie einen Artikel schreiben, in dem Sie darüber informieren, inwiefern sich die Arbeitsbedingungen in Bangladeschs Textilfabriken verbessert haben.
Sie haben den folgenden Artikel gelesen und notieren sich auf Deutsch Stichpunkte über die Verbesserungen, die nach der Katastrophe in Bangladesch gemacht wurden.

Two years after Rana Plaza, have conditions improved in Bangladesh's factories?

On 24 April 2013, an eight-story garment factory collapsed in Dhaka, the capital of Bangladesh. The building's fall killed 1,134 people and injured hundreds of others. The Rana Plaza tragedy was not caused by an earthquake or a terrorist attack, but rather by poor construction and a lack of oversight – and, in some ways, by a growing global desire for more cheap fashion.

It's been two years since the Rana Plaza tragedy, and although much remains to be done to ensure the rights and safety of workers in Bangladesh's still-booming garment industry, progress has been made. Global brands including *H&M*, *Mango*, *Primark*, the *Gap* and *Walmart*, among a dozen others, have contributed $21.5 m to the *Rana Plaza Donors Trust Fund*, which was set up to award compensation to victims and their families. [...]

But the real change will come in the form of improvements to worker safety and worker's rights. According to Reddy [*Anm. Bangladeshi director for the International Labour Organization, ILO*], Dhaka's permitting offices have simply not kept pace with its booming garment industry, leading to a situation in which factories were being given permits without so much as a site visit, much less monitoring.

That has begun to change since the Rana Plaza collapse. According to Reddy, out of 3,508 factories identified as exporting clothing from Bangladesh, almost 75 % have gone through building fire and safety assessments. As a result, 35 factories have been closed for failing to comply with structural integrity standards.

"That is not good news, necessarily, but what's important is to recognize that we might have actually averted some building problems and accidents by closing down these factories," Reddy said, "and putting the remaining factories through the remediation process" that requires building owners to fix various building safety issues. [...]

Several brands and retailers are playing an active role in addressing worker safety issues in Bangladesh, according to Reddy, in terms of both paying for factories to be upgraded and working with government agencies and nongovernmental organizations to draft guidelines and strategies for improving the lot of garment workers.

However, those commitments are set to end in 2018. "So we need to focus on how to continue this work, train monitoring staff, and ensure that capacity is built into the local authorities," Reddy said.

One problem that has yet to be addressed, according to Reddy, is the capacity issue in *Dhaka's Capital Development Authority*. The Authority approves building permits and is supposed to monitor construction to ensure that buildings are built according to the approved design. "Currently they do not really monitor," Reddy said. "They grant permits and then don't monitor, because they just don't have enough monitoring staff. That was one of the problems with Rana Plaza – they were approved for six floors and built eight. That's still a weak link and we're asking the government to step up."

Although the *ILO* and other NGOs are pleased with the progress that has been made on worker safety, worker rights issues have lagged behind. At the end of 2012, there were 122 unions in Bangladesh's garment industry and they represented less than 3 % of workers. [...]

Today there are 437 unions, representing nearly 5 % of workers in the industry. Part of the remediation plans that came out of talks immediately following the Rana Plaza collapse was the need to establish worker safety committees at the city's factories, so that employees would have a place to voice concerns about workplace safety. So far, those committees have not been formed because the government has been slow to draft policies for their creation. [...]

Attention has been good and bad for Bangladesh's garment industry, according to Reddy. On the one hand, it has spurred international brands to take a keen interest in the country, supplying funding, time and ideas to improving the garment industry there. On the other, it has created pressure for the industry to improve rapidly.

"All these issues evolved over the course of the past 30 years, but people wanted to see them fixed in months," Reddy said. "Some people felt like, 'Why is everyone focused on Bangladesh when there are a lot of other exporting countries that don't meet these international standards?'"

The Rana Plaza reforms have not touched 40 % of the country's factories, and these tend to be the facilities that are exporting to various countries through small brands and retailers.

The hope now is that the world will continue to pay attention to these issues, and that smaller companies and brands, not just the big players with reputations to protect, will support reform as well.

(798 words)

Quelle: Amy Westervelt, *The Guardian*, April 24, 2015, www.theguardian.com.

C | Textproduktion

3 Materialgestützter Aufsatz

Write a composition about the following topic.
- **Use the information of at least three of the given materials.**
- **Name which ones you are using.**
- **Make use of your own ideas.**
- **Do not write three separate compositions but one covering all the materials chosen.**

The integration of immigrants is one of the most widely discussed topics in Europe. Discuss the chances and problems of integrating immigrants into society and state your point of view.

1

Welsh youngsters learn to rethink racism

[...] The white men on the screen are shouting, fists jabbing the air. "Allah, Allah, who the fuck is Allah?" and "If you all hate Pakis, clap your hands". The young people watching are silent, serious. "It's embarrassing," they say afterwards. "They are making us all look bad."

The men in the film are from the *Welsh Defence League* – a spin-off of the far-right *English Defence League* – and the teenagers watching them are taking part in the *Think Project*, a three-day course aimed at stopping young white people in south Wales from getting involved in far-right extremism.

The project was created by the Swansea-based *Ethnic Youth Support Team (EYST)* in response to the racist and Islamophobic abuse experienced by the organisation's ethnic minority clients. In south Wales there were 1,421 racially motivated attacks last year. [...]

The project links with agencies working with teenagers excluded from school or young people not in work, education or training and delivers the course as part of their programmes. The material covered is wide-ranging: racism, migration, asylum, extremism, religion, human rights. [...]

"We aim to get a conversation going," explains Chris Mort, who runs the course with colleague Nicky Nijjer. "No-one listens to these kids at school. They have never had the chance to debate and have their views heard. This is about including them, never putting them down. We want to get them to be a bit more political, build them up a bit." [...]

(247 words)

Quelle: Laura Smith, *The Guardian*, May 27, 2014, www.theguardian.com.

2

Ehrenamt-Projekt in Köln

Dass sich Deutsche für Flüchtlinge und Zuwanderer engagieren, ist ziemlich normal. Umgekehrt kommt das eher selten vor. Im Kölner Stadtbezirk Kalk helfen Zuwanderer Alteingesessenen. Und lernen so eine Menge.

Köln, Seniorenheim St. Theodor, Aufenthaltsraum: Neben einer alten Frau mit lockigem Haar sitzt Jakleen R. Die 31-Jährige liest aus einer Zeitschrift vor. […] Seit einigen Monaten kommt sie jede Woche für zwei Stunden in das Altenheim und kümmert sich um die alten Menschen. Ehrenamtlich. […]

„Viele Flüchtlinge und Zuwanderer wünschen sich mehr Kontakt zu – in Anführungsstrichen – echten Deutschen“, erzählt Elizaveta Khan. Sie leitet das „Integrationshaus“ in Kalk. „Ungefähr ein Viertel aller Teilnehmer aus jedem Kurs sind sofort zur Freiwilligenarbeit bereit.“ Deshalb hat der Verein vor zwei Jahren gemeinsam mit der Bürgerstiftung „KalkGestalten“ das Ehrenamts-Projekt „Sei dabei! Für dich, für mich, für alle!“ auf die Beine gestellt. Ziel ist es, Flüchtlinge zu motivieren, sich so rasch wie möglich ehrenamtlich zu betätigen. „Denn sonst gehen viele Kursteilnehmer nach den Sprachkursen wieder in ihre Familien zurück und haben keine Chance Deutsche zu treffen“, meint Rainer Kreke, Sprecher der Stiftung „KalkGestalten“. „Und so bekommen sie dann keinen Zugang zur deutschen Kultur. Die Freiwilligenarbeit kann das ändern.“ […]

Der „Nebeneffekt“ der Ehrenarbeit ist unbezahlbar. „Die Leute werden beim Einkaufen von ‚Deutschen‘ erkannt, man unterhält sich und wer weiß, was daraus erwächst. Sie haben nicht mehr das Gefühl passiv zu sein, sondern können mitgestalten und fühlen sich dadurch auf Augenhöhe. Das stärkt ihr Selbstbewusstsein“, hat Elizaveta Khan beobachtet. […]

(245 Wörter)

Quelle: Lisa von Prondzinski, 25.07.2015, www1.wdr.de.

3

4

A. **"I had a young person doing warehouse work when really he could be doing much better. His English was really good but they were the only ones who would accept his permission to work."**
Quelle: Swaliha Bax, case worker at the *Dost Centre for Young Refugees and Migrants* in east London, www.theguardian.com, September 15, 2015.

B. **"The real issue for the future is the very large numbers of low-paid immigrants from eastern Europe. [...] The [...] report does not take into account – no doubt for good reason – future health costs as migrants get older nor the pension bill, which is huge."**
Quelle: Sir Andrew Green, *Migration Watch, BBC News*, www.bbc.com, November 5, 2013.

C. **"These kids [of first-generation immigrants] have grown up here, but just because they have the wrong status they are being denied education. It should be a fundamental right, not a privilege."**
Quelle: Rupa Huq, MP, www.theguardian.com, June 24, 2015.

D. **"This [survey of British schoolchildren] is not evidence of widespread racism among young people but it is clear there is a large degree of anxiety – often based on inaccurate information – about what is happening in their communities and about their own futures."**
Quelle: Prof Hilary Pilkington, University of Manchester, www.theguardian.com, May 19, 2015.

What determines successful integration? 5

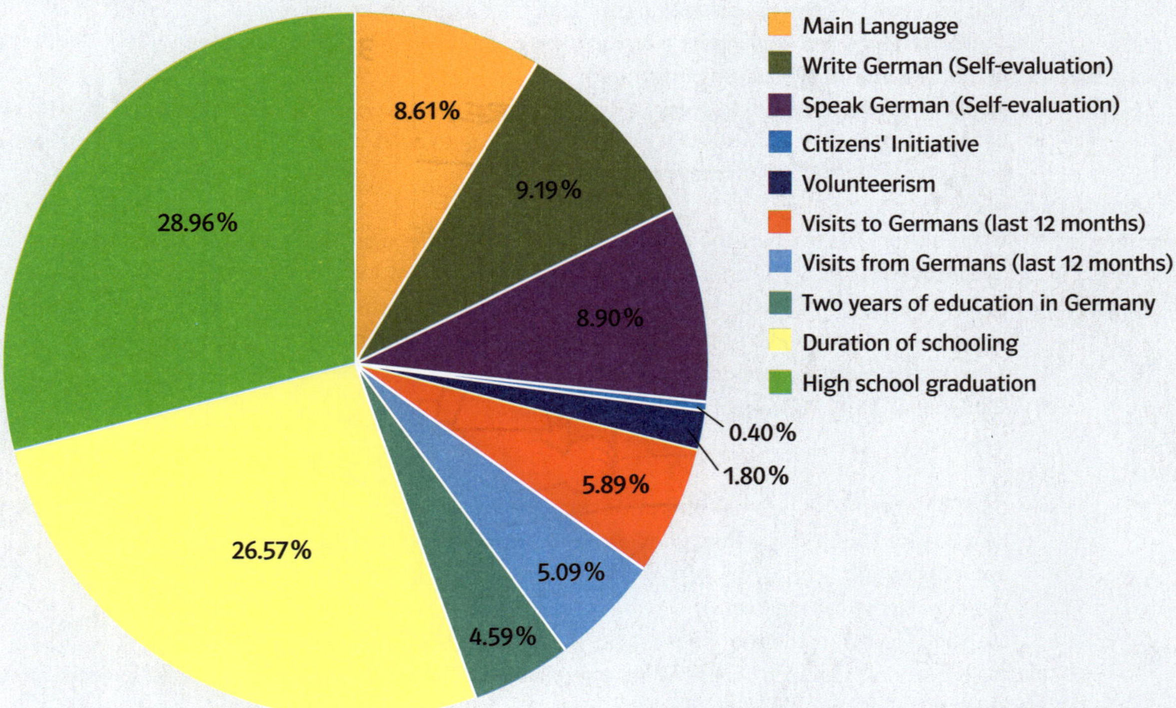

Datenquelle/Data source: German ministry for Migration and Refugees

Audioscripts

3.15 Unit 11, 1a

Radio presenter: Good afternoon. This is James Stoke from *Radio Sheffield* bringing you "Job profile". In today's programme we are going to be talking about apprenticeships for young people. In the studio we have Jack Swinton from Sheffield who is already doing an apprenticeship. First Jack, tell us a bit about how you became an apprentice?

Jack: Well, it took a while before I actually decided to do an apprenticeship. You see, while I was at school, I was lucky enough to get an offer of a professional contract with Sheffield United football club. I was only 17 and the idea of getting paid to do something I loved seemed like a great idea at first. But it takes a lot of time and luck to get into the first team and then your chances of actually making it big in football are very small. I talked things over with my parents and friends and decided to reject the offer and continue going to school.

Radio presenter: So how did you find your apprenticeship?

Jack: Well, like I said, I was still at school doing my GSCEs when my class tutor suggested I look into apprenticeships. I have always been interested in building things, so I looked at the National Apprenticeship website for opportunities in the building sector. In the end, after discussing everything with my parents, I decided that a construction apprenticeship would be the best thing for me.

Radio presenter: And you were obviously successful in your search for an employer, too.

Jack: That's right. I started working for a construction company here in Sheffield in 2016.

Radio presenter: And how is your apprenticeship organized?

Jack: I work on the building site four days a week and go to college on the other day. The hours at work can be long, but I enjoy it there. What I like most is helping to build something from the start and then seeing the end result. That's really satisfying.

Radio presenter: And what about college?

Jack: That's ok, too. The teachers there are very helpful. One of them advised me to try to get higher qualifications later. So, when I finish my apprenticeship I think I will go to evening classes to get my BTEC in construction. The course takes two years. If I'm successful, I could possibly go on to university to study civil engineering. At the moment I'm very pleased with my choice of apprenticeship. Now I know what I really want to do with my life.

Radio presenter: That sounds great, Jack. What do you want ...?

3.16 Unit 11, 1b

Radio presenter: Good afternoon. This is James Stoke from *Radio Sheffield* bringing you "Job profile". In the studio today we have Samantha Young from Sheffield. Now, Samantha, what made you decide to do an apprenticeship?

Samantha: Hi there. Please call me Sam.

Radio presenter: Ok, Sam. So what made you choose to do an apprenticeship?

Sam: Well at school I just didn't know what career I wanted. The only thing I knew was that I enjoyed being creative.

Radio presenter: So how did you find the right apprenticeship for you?

Sam: I went to the job centre here in Sheffield and the people there said I should look at the National Apprenticeship website. I took their advice because I didn't really have any other choice. I didn't want to be unemployed and end up without any qualifications.

Radio presenter: And you were obviously successful.

Sam: That's right. I found an offer of a very interesting apprenticeship on the website. It included work experience with a special effects company in Manchester which has contracts with several national TV companies. The company is based in Media City, in Manchester because that's where the *BBC* and *ITV* have their northern headquarters. So, after going through the application procedure, you know, letter of application, CV, job interview and so on, I was lucky enough to be offered the apprenticeship.

Radio presenter: So you moved to Manchester then, didn't you?

Sam: Yes, I did. It's too far to travel every day from Sheffield. But the company helped me to find a flat, which I share with two other apprentices.

Radio presenter: And how is your apprenticeship organized?

Sam: Well, I go to a college in Manchester which offers a special course for people wanting to work in creative and digital media. I spend about three months at the college and then I do six weeks' work experience at the company. Then I go back to college for the next part and so on for the next two years. I have to take an exam at the end of the two years.

Radio presenter: And what do you like best about the apprenticeship?

Sam: Well, although the college course is fine, I find the work in the company more interesting. You see, I've already been involved in one extremely exciting project.

Radio presenter: Tell us about it.

Sam: Sure. I've been working on a TV film for the *BBC*. I helped to create scenes with explosives using atmospheric smoke and fire effects. That was fun.

Radio presenter: You seem to be really happy with your choice of apprenticeship.

Sam: Yes I am. And I can definitely recommend an apprenticeship to any young people listening to the programme. I would also highly recommend looking at the National Apprenticeship website. You are sure to find something that interests you. Another thing, I would …

3.17 **Unit 12, 1a**

Radio presenter: I'm Melanie Moore and you're listening to *Channel 555*. Today we are going to talk about the effect that the media has on young people. In the studio today we have two students from a local college here in Manchester, Christina Waites and Mark Donaldson. First of all, Christina, how much, would you say, do media like TV influence you?

Christina: Well when I was younger, say 13 or 14, I used to watch about six hours of TV a day and I guess I was influenced quite a lot by it. But now I'm 19 and I only watch about two hours in the evening, mostly soaps or talent shows. I spend most of my time on social networking websites or watch videos on the Internet that friends have said are cool.

Radio presenter: And what about you, Mark?

Mark: Well, I don't watch much TV, either. The only difference to Christina is that I watch about 6 or 7 hours of sports programmes a week. Apart from that I play online games with friends and watch my favourite series online.

Radio presenter: Several surveys have found that a lot of the media that young people use have a negative effect on them, especially when it comes to body image. What do you think about that, Christina?

Christina: Well I really don't like the way young women are portrayed in the media. In a lot of TV programmes the girls look like models or pop stars. We 'normal girls' get the feeling that we should be like them, and if we are not, then we think we're inferior. And another thing I don't like is the way alcohol is shown. The commercials show drinking alcohol as a "cool" thing to do. As a result I think a lot of teens who want to be "cool" often drink too much and can even end up binge-drinking.

Radio presenter: Well, Mark, do you agree with Christina about the negative effect of the media?

Mark: Yes I do. A lot of violence is shown by the media. When I think of some of the games my friends play that show murder, rape, armed robberies and so on, it is not surprising if young people lose touch with reality. They can become used to violence and tend to think such behaviour is normal and even become violent themselves.

Radio presenter: So what do you think can be done, Mark?

Mark: In my opinion, what's most important is to teach children and young people how to deal with modern media, and especially with social networking websites. Just think how these media influence the way that we, and children especially, see the world. I think such platforms should be open to everybody, but at the same time there should be some sort of control on what can be shown on these types of media.

Christina: And I think you should just turn …

3.18 **Unit 12, 1b**

Professor: Good morning ladies and gentlemen. Today's lecture is about the effects of advertising on teenagers. As I'm sure you're aware, the flood of commercials on television, and also on the Internet and on social media platforms, is specifically aimed at the teenage population. After all teenagers today have huge spending power. The companies which want to sell their products use these media because they know that teenagers nowadays have this spending power and that teenagers spend a lot of their time either online or watching TV.

According to a recent study carried out in the UK, teenagers spend most of their money on music. So, it is not surprising that advertising for the music industry on the TV, the radio and, of course on social networking platforms, targets teenagers. The same study reported that of the eight hundred teenagers interviewed 95% had a television set in their room. So you see, the media is everywhere and companies have teenagers in their sights.

There is, of course, no doubt that advertising in the media can have a negative effect on the development of young people's behaviour. For example, young people see commercials portraying cigarettes and alcohol as being worthwhile and cool. It's not surprising that we now have so many under-age drinkers and smokers.

The temptation is, however, to think that companies only use the media to promote risky behaviour to teenagers. It is true that the negative issues get our attention, but there are positive effects as well. Some companies are starting to use the media to promote positive messages to teens.

A good example can be found in handout number four: You can see how one company has taken its responsibility to young people seriously when using the media for its advertising. The company has decided to put self-esteem into the foreground. They have chosen real women and girls with 'normal bodies' as models for their advertising campaigns rather than really thin models. In this way young people experience a positive feedback and don't feel guilty when they don't have a body like the models in most adverts.

Another positive step towards dealing with the media is certainly in the hands of the government. As I said before teenagers spend a lot of their time using various forms of media. Here the governments could and should take a leading role by banning commercials which involve cigarettes and alcohol.

It is of course impossible to prevent teenagers from coming into contact with advertising, but I would say …

3.19 **Unit 13, 1a**

Radio presenter: This is *Radio AIR2* broadcasting from Southampton and I'm Celine Jones. Today on "Teens Talk" we are going to focus on the topic of student debt. I am pleased to welcome Mike Rowling from the *Citizens Advice Bureau* who can give us some expert advice on financial problems. I'd also like to welcome Debbie and Kieran, two students at Southampton University. Let's start with you Kieran and Debbie. Could you tell our listeners something about your financial problems? Debbie?

Debbie: Yes, we are both in our last year at university and we have to study a lot for our final exams. The problem is that we just don't have time for our part-time jobs and unfortunately we've gotten into financial difficulties.

Kieran: That's right. While we had our part-time jobs we could live quite comfortably – we could pay for food and clothes, and even have a night out now and again.

Debbie: That's right. We could even afford to go on holiday last summer. We got a cheap flight to Ibiza and the hotel was quite basic.

Kieran: But the problem was that food and drinks were separate. And before we went we didn't realize that Ibiza is quite expensive.

Debbie: When we got back here to Southampton we had run up quite a bit of debt on our credit cards. And of course we still had our running costs – you know rent, electricity and food.

Kieran: Yes. And when I think about the student loans we got for our studies I just don't know how I am going to pay all that money back. Most students end up with a load of debts before they start earning real money.

Radio presenter: Right. I think it's time to bring in Mike Rowling. Mike, what advice can you give Debbie and Kieran?

Mike: Well first of all Kieran and Debbie, you should know that you are not alone with this problem. The average student in the UK owes about 20,000 pounds after his or her studies. About half of that is the student loan. On top of that a lot of students have to pay back bank loans and any money they may have borrowed from their families.

Debbie: OK. But what would you advise us to do?

Mike: Well the first thing I would suggest that you do to sort out your financial problems is to make two lists. On the first list you should write down all of the places where you have debts. Let's call it the debts list. You should put the debts in order of priority, starting with the debts which must be paid back first. Then you should make a second list. Let's call it the expenses list. You should write down how much you spend in a normal month. That can help you to work out where you could cut back on your spending. In this way you would save some money to pay off your credit card debts.

Radio presenter: That sounds good. Mike, what about…

3.20 Unit 13, 1b

Radio presenter: Hello everyone. I'm Jessie Sanders and you're listening to *Radio Manchester*. Welcome to this week's programme, "It's your turn". Today we want to discuss child poverty in the UK. I'm pleased to welcome Mary Wintour from the city council to the programme. Mary, what exactly does it mean to be poor in the UK?

Mary: Well, it is not so easy to answer that question. The current definition of relative poverty is when someone's income is 60 per cent lower than the average household income in the UK. But please let me add that being poor is not only about money. Of course, everyone here in the UK must have access to basic necessities such as running water, food and clothing as well as a telephone and heating. However, I am of the opinion that we need to add some other indicators to measure poverty, especially when we talk about child poverty.

Radio presenter: What other factors do you have in mind?

Mary: I believe that we should also think about the possibility of letting children participate in cultural activities, such as visits to the zoo or museums. These are so called 'non-material resources', which help children to fully integrate into society. We shouldn't forget that these activities are real life chances for children to improve their living conditions. They also keep children from poor families from becoming socially isolated.

Radio presenter: So what causes child poverty here in the UK?

Mary: Basically, child poverty is often due to the fact that one or both parents are unemployed. However poverty may also arise from parents having low-paid jobs. Families that live off state benefits or have high childcare costs can find themselves sliding into poverty. Further causes of child poverty are family breakdowns, and alcohol and drug-addicted parents.

Radio presenter: What consequences do poor children have to face?

Mary: Unfortunately, children from poor families are less likely to do well at school. Very often they have to take on additional responsibilities in the home, for example they have to babysit younger siblings and so have less time to socialize or learn for school. These children are also almost three times as likely to suffer from mental health problems when they grow up. In addition, poor children are more likely to be unemployed or have unskilled jobs later. So they will probably be poorly paid in later life. It's a vicious circle that they can't escape so easily.

Radio presenter: But there must be something that the government can do to end child poverty in the UK.

Mary: Of course, there are several measures that the government must take. First, they must lift children out of poverty by helping parents to find work and by increasing the minimum wage. Second, the government must improve access to education services and so reduce the risk of poor children becoming poor adults.

Radio presenter: Mary, why do you think …?

3.21 Unit 14, 1a

Radio presenter: Good morning. This is Jason Green on the "Energy Show". Last week we reported from the European climate conference. Government officials there expressed the view that there should be a greater focus on green technologies to help solve the problem of climate change.

In the studio today I have two experts whose companies are doing innovative work on new green technologies. Our first guest is Susan Miller from "Severn Soft Cells". Could you tell our listeners a little about the latest product that your company has developed, Susan?

Susan: Of course. At the present time we at "Severn Soft Cells" are developing a new generation of solar cells which includes a transparent solar cell.

Radio presenter: Could you give our listeners an idea of how the transparent solar cell works?

Susan: Well, just imagine a solar cell that looks like a piece of glass that is only one thousandth of a millimeter thick. This glass or cell transmits light that is invisible to the human eye and at the same time it converts ultraviolet light into electricity. This power which the solar cells supply can be used to extend the battery life of electronic devices considerably. Hopefully, one day we can use this transparent solar cell as the sole energy source for portable electronic devices, such as mobile phones and tablets. And another advantage of these new solar cells is that they are clear, in fact they look exactly like normal glass. So, in future, windows could even be made from these solar cells. The windows would then generate enough solar energy to supply appliances in the house.

Radio presenter: When do you intend to start selling your transparent solar cells?

Susan: Let's say in about three or four years' time. At the moment we only have a prototype, which already reduces the time between battery charges on mobile phones considerably. We are sure that our cells will replace rechargeable batteries in mobile phones completely in the future.

Radio presenter: That sounds promising. And now, John Skinner, your company is working on a similar project, isn't it?

John: Yes, that's right. We at "RecycleMore" are developing biodegradable batteries at the moment. At present about 22,000 tonnes of household batteries end up on landfill sites every year. And recycling rates are extremely low – only about 10% of household batteries are in fact recycled. So my company has decided to look into the possibility of creating more efficient, biodegradable batteries that are environmentally friendly. We are working on a battery made of a wood-based substance called aerogel. Our target markets are portable computing and in-car electronic manufacturers. To give you an idea of how innovative this battery is let me tell you that the batteries that are on the market at the moment are only made of about 4% recyclable parts. Our aerogel-based batteries would be almost 100% recyclable.

Radio presenter: Thanks John. That is quite impressive. Well, listeners these are just a few of the energy saving innovations which have the potential to make energy production greener. What do you think about ...?

3.22 **Unit 14, 1b**

Radio presenter: Welcome to *Radio 606*. I'm Phil Flute and on today's programme we are going to discuss what makes life here in London so stressful. From noise to pollution – the causes of stress in big cities are manifold. I have two guests in the studio today, Indira Khan and Tony Green, who want to talk about the things that make their lives here in London stressful. Indira, what makes your life in a big city like London so stressful?

Indira: Well, what makes me feel particularly stressed is the air pollution. You see, I suffer from asthma and I just hate breathing in all the fumes from the traffic here. I can't avoid it because my work is in the centre of London. Another thing which makes me feel stressed is that there are so many people living and working here that they start to feel anonymous. And when people feel anonymous, that gives them a "not my problem" attitude. This attitude leads them to bad habits like dropping their rubbish on the streets or spitting chewing gum on the ground. You see, I get very angry when I see people not caring for the environment.

Radio presenter: What about you, Tony? You work in London, too. What would you say makes your life here stressful?

Tony: The main thing that affects my stress levels is the constant pushing and jostling on the trains, on the tube, on the buses and even on escalators. Everybody seems to be in a rush. Even in their lunch breaks people are jostling one another in the shops and cafés. I think that if we all relaxed a little more we would get where we wanted to go – maybe it would take a little longer but we would be happier.

Indira: That's right. When I think of how I travel to work every day ... I leave home in north London at seven in the morning and run to the bus stop to catch the number 14 bus to the nearest tube station. Then I jump off the bus, sprint up the hill to the tube station and run down the escalator to catch a Northern Line train to King's Cross. When I get there it's the same story – run, run, run to get into work for 8 o'clock.

Tony: Yes. Since my workplace has shifted from a small town just outside London to Oxford Street in the city centre my health has suffered.

Radio presenter: Would you mind telling us how?

Tony: Well about three months ago I started getting pains in my chest. It got so bad I went to the doctor and he told me that I was suffering from stress-related heart problems. Nothing acute, but I have to take medicine to help me combat the stress.

Radio presenter: What would you both say about ...?

3.23 **Unit 15, 1a**

Radio presenter: Good morning, I'm Susanna Lindgard and you are listening to *Radio Manchester*. Welcome to today's programme, "Can mass tourism be sustainable?" We have two experts with us to discuss this topic. Our first guest is Oliver Parkin who is an expert on the effects of mass tourism and Anna Moorhouse, a journalist who has written a lot about this topic. If I could start with you, Oliver, why should we be so concerned about the effect the tourist industry has on our world today?

Oliver: Well in many countries tourism is the primary source of employment and we should also bear in mind that about 1.8 billion tourists will be travelling to foreign countries within the next 15 years. That shows you the scale of the tourist industry and the effect it has on us all.

Radio presenter: So where is this development leading us to?

Oliver: To big, big problems. Obviously we as consumers have become addicted to the promise of cheap flights and inexpensive hotels. However, our holiday choices are often not good for the environment. If we were completely honest, these choices are helping to damage the environment. Just think of the emissions a flight to your holiday destination causes. And we shouldn't forget the residents of the tourist hotspots either. Most of the local people welcomed the first hotels, but now a lot of them find that holiday resorts do not only bring more employment to the region. In fact, the cost of land, houses and even water have increased considerably for many local residents. Sadly, mass tourism doesn't always benefit everybody.

Radio presenter: So what should we do? Anna Moorhouse, you are a journalist who has done a lot of research into ways of making tourism more sustainable. Can you tell us a little about your findings, Anna?

Anna: First, let me take up the point Oliver has just made about the local people's attitude to tourist development. I went to Thailand last year where I interviewed Manee Luang, a successful businesswoman who set up her first holiday hotel in Phuket about 30 years ago. She told me that she first talked to representatives of the local community about their jobs and the handicrafts that were made and sold locally. After those talks she decided to offer local craftsmen the chance to sell their products in her hotel. That is what I call a real contribution to bringing employment and prosperity to tourist resorts beyond the hotel doors. By the way, Manee Luang has become so successful that she now owns 90 hotels all over Southeast Asia.

Radio presenter: Well, that certainly sounds like a formula for success. In recent years sustainable tourism has become a catchphrase among travel agencies, but to what extent is the 'sustainable' tourism in glossy travel brochures really sustainable, Oliver?

Oliver: Well, I must admit that mainstream mass tourism is only starting to manage the social and environmental problems it has caused in some parts of the world. Nevertheless, as Anna's example shows, it is possible, even for large hotel chains, to make tourism sustainable.

Radio presenter: Anna, what would you say about … ?

3.24 **Unit 15, 1b**

Adviser: As an adviser from a human rights organization I would like to inform you about the work that we are currently doing as regards child exploitation in the tourist industry. With the growth of digital technology we can now get access to cheap flights and hotel accommodation all over the world. As a result, the tourist industry has grown at an astonishing speed over the last few years. However, the downside of this development is that holidaymakers – especially in developing countries – are brought into contact with children who are at risk of crimes such as child trafficking. A key point for us is the role of the tourist industry in employment. We are, of course, in favour of the development of jobs in the hotel business for young local people. However, these young people are also often at risk. They frequently have to work long hours, sometimes in dangerous conditions. We focus on helping to create decent working conditions and on promoting the rights of young hotel workers. In this respect, I am pleased to say, a number of leading hotel chains and tour operators are now working hand in hand with us.

Before I go on, I must stress that the leading tour operators are certainly NOT directly responsible for child sex tourism in any way and that a lot of these companies and hotel chains help us in our work. They help us by reporting any cases they may be aware of. Moreover, in cooperation with several leading tour operators we are able to run a programme of e-learning workshops to provide extra training for hotel staff. The modules are all based on real-life cases and are designed to teach staff members at the hotels how to notice and deal with cases of child exploitation that they see in their hotel. This programme has been quite successful.

In quite a few countries where mass tourism has expanded and the infrastructure for tourism is being developed you can often see children involved in activities such as the construction of new hotels or in building roads. Here again, we have started to assist governments and the tourist industry in updating guidelines and standards to protect children. We have a long way to go but I can say with some certainty that we are beginning to get to the heart of these problems with the help of most of the tourist industry.

Bildquellennachweis

Cover 1 Avenue Images GmbH (Westend61), Hamburg; **Cover 2** Getty Images (Corbis Documentary), München; **4** iStockphoto (monkeybusinessimages), Calgary, Alberta; **5** iStockphoto (Robert Churchill), Calgary, Alberta; **9** Fotolia.com (rookie72), New York; **10** Fotolia.com (.shock), New York; **11** iStockphoto (JMichl), Calgary, Alberta; **12.1** Fotolia.com (Christopher Jones), New York; **12.2** iStockphoto (encrier), Calgary, Alberta; **14.1** iStockphoto (Maxiphoto), Calgary, Alberta; **14.2** iStockphoto (iprogressman), Calgary, Alberta; **14.3** iStockphoto (Ellica_S), Calgary, Alberta; **14.4** iStockphoto (carlopops), Calgary, Alberta; **14.5** iStockphoto (Sean2008), Calgary, Alberta; **14.6** shutterstock.com (Feraru Nicolae), New York, NY; **14.7** Thinkstock (Jupiterimages), München; **17.1** Fotolia.com (bertys30), New York; **17.2** shutterstock.com (BigLike Images), New York, NY; **17.3** shutterstock.com (Lucky Business), New York, NY; **17.4** shutterstock.com (Joana Lopes), New York, NY; **17.5** Fotolia.com (Masson), New York; **17.6** shutterstock.com (Supri Suharjoto), New York, NY; **17.7** iStockphoto (wavebreakmedia), Calgary, Alberta; **17.8** Fotolia.com (Nathalie P), New York; **17.9** dreamstime.com (Diademimages), Brentwood, TN; **19** Fotolia.com (auremar), New York; **20.1** Fotolia.com, New York; **20.2** shutterstock.com (Lucky Business), New York, NY; **22** shutterstock.com (Thiago Leite), New York, NY; **23** iStockphoto (Lisa-Blue), Calgary, Alberta; **25** Fotolia.com (contrastwerkstatt), New York; **27.1** dreamstime.com (Maxexphoto), Brentwood, TN; **27.2** iStockphoto (Pali Rao), Calgary, Alberta; **27.3** dreamstime.com (Norman Chan), Brentwood, TN; **28** dreamstime.com (Indos82), Brentwood, TN; **29** shutterstock.com (Gabriel Georgescu), New York, NY; **30.1** shutterstock.com (Robert Kneschke), New York, NY; **30.2** Thinkstock (Creatas), München; **32** iStockphoto (Tom Nulens), Calgary, Alberta; **33** iStockphoto (sergeyryzhov), Calgary, Alberta; **36** shutterstock.com (Jeff Gynane), New York, NY; **37** iStockphoto (mapodile), Calgary, Alberta; **38.1** shutterstock.com (goodluz), New York, NY; **38.2** shutterstock.com (Peter Bernik), New York, NY; **39** shutterstock.com (Dikiiy), New York, NY; **40.1**; **40.2** www.CartoonStock.com (Chris Wildt), Bath; **41** iStockphoto (Antonio_Diaz), Calgary, Alberta; **42** iStockphoto (AlbertPego), Calgary, Alberta; **43** iStockphoto (PeopleImages), Calgary, Alberta; **44.1** Fotolia.com (Luca Oleastri), New York; **44.2** Imago (Arnulf Hettrich), Berlin; **45** Thinkstock (monkeybusinessimages), München; **46** shutterstock.com (wavebreakmedia), New York, NY; **47.1** Fotolia.com (redlinevector), New York; **47.2**; **47.3**; **47.4** Fotolia.com (ksenia_bravo), New York; **47.5** shutterstock.com (file404), New York, NY; **47.6** shutterstock.com (Arcady), New York, NY; **47.7** shutterstock.com (PandaVector), New York, NY; **47.8** Fotolia.com (007NATALIIA), New York; **47.9** shutterstock.com (jiunn), New York, NY; **49** Fotolia.com (grafxart), New York; **51** iStockphoto (Lisa Kyle Young), Calgary, Alberta; **52** iStockphoto (Hung_Chung_Chih), Calgary, Alberta; **53** shutterstock.com (Claudia Paulussen), New York, NY; **56** Fotolia.com (lapas77), New York; **57** Fotolia.com (alain wacquier), New York; **58.1** Imago (Lovell), Berlin; **58.2** Fotolia.com (dieter76), New York; **58.3** Ullstein Bild GmbH (Imagebroker.net), Berlin; **58.4** iStockphoto (kynny), Calgary, Alberta; **58.5** Thinkstock (iStockphoto), München; **59** Fotolia.com (sebastianreuter), New York; **60** iStockphoto (mikkelwilliam), Calgary, Alberta; **61** Fotolia.com (bildergala), New York; **62** Fotolia.com (LuckyImages), New York; **64.1** iStockphoto, Calgary, Alberta; **64.2** iStockphoto (3DSculptor), Calgary, Alberta; **65** Fotolia.com (Xavier MARCHANT), New York; **66** Fotolia.com (Hendrik Schwartz), New York; **67** Fotolia.com (Esther Hildebrandt), New York; **68** iStockphoto (Steve Debenport), Calgary, Alberta; **69** Fotolia.com (Francesco83), New York; **71** iStockphoto (andresr), Calgary, Alberta; **73** shutterstock.com (Dmitry Chulov), New York, NY; **74** shutterstock.com (Pablo Rogat), New York, NY; **76** iStockphoto (Fertnig), Calgary, Alberta; **77** shutterstock.com (FXQuadro), New York, NY; **78** Fotolia.com (Vospalej), New York; **81** www.CartoonStock.com (Mike Puckett), Bath; **83** Fotolia.com (aalutcenko), New York; **84** iStockphoto (OJO_Images), Calgary, Alberta; **85** iStockphoto (OJO_Images), Calgary, Alberta; **86** iStockphoto (anyaberkut), Calgary, Alberta; **87** iStockphoto (Wavebreakmedia), Calgary, Alberta; **88** shutterstock.com (Zagrean Viorel), New York, NY; **89.1** shutterstock.com (Lisa Kolbasa), New York, NY; **89.2** Fotolia.com (Annatamila), New York; **89.3** shutterstock.com (Samo Trebizan), New York, NY; **89.5** Fotolia.com (zephyr_p), New York; **89.6** iStockphoto (Dmitry Idanov), Calgary, Alberta; **89.7**; **89.8** Fotolia.com (merfin), New York; **89.9** Fotolia.com (muchmania), New York; **89.10** Fotolia.com (iconicbestiary), New York; **90** Fotolia.com (lightpoet), New York; **90.1** Fotolia.com (ViewApart), New York; **91** iStockphoto (manaemedia), Calgary, Alberta; **92** iStockphoto (ClarkandCompany), Calgary, Alberta; **94** shutterstock.com (mauro_grigollo), New York, NY; **95.1** iStockphoto (PeopleImages), Calgary, Alberta; **95.2** iStockphoto (Andy Tuohy), Calgary, Alberta; **95.3** Fotolia.com (lovemask), New York; **96** iStockphoto (lzf), Calgary, Alberta; **97** Picture-Alliance (JOKER), Frankfurt; **98** iStockphoto (Linda Yolanda), Calgary, Alberta; **98.4** iStockphoto (franckreporter), Calgary, Alberta; **99** shutterstock.com (Maridav), New York, NY; **100** Fotolia.com (Tony Bowler), New York; **101** www.CartoonStock.com (Chris Madden), Bath; **102** Fotolia.com (Syda Productions), New York; **103** shutterstock.com (JuliusKielaitis), New York, NY; **104** iStockphoto (vgajic), Calgary, Alberta; **105** Fotolia.com (kengmerry), New York; **106.1** Fotolia.com (zozzzzo), New York; **106.2** www.CartoonStock.com (Grizelda), Bath; **108** iStockphoto (Maciej Bledowski), Calgary, Alberta; **110** Fotolia.com (Jörg Lantelme), New York; **111** iStockphoto (Rawpixel Ltd), Calgary, Alberta; **112** www.CartoonStock.com (Piero Tonin), Bath

Textquellennachweis

79 The Guardian.com; **80** Zeit online, 2010; **81** Telegraph, 2014; **81** © 2009, Guardian News & Media Ltd.; **86** © 2015, Guardian News & Media Ltd.; **87** © 2013, Guardian News & Media Ltd.; **88** Zeit Campus; **89** Mark Watson in: The Guardian, 19th March 2015; **89** Jonathan Bryan in: The Telegraph, 29th Julz 2015; **89** Dr. Jennifer Wilby in: The Guardian, 26th August 2015; **89** Stefan Wathan in: The Telepgraph, 18th July 2015; **92** © 2015, Guardian News & Media Ltd.; **93** © 2011, Guardian News & Media Ltd.; **94** n-tv.de , ppo/dpa; **95** BBC News Website: http://www.bbc.com/news/uk-22867315; **95** © 2010, Guardian News & Media Ltd.; **95** BBC News Website, http://www.bbc.com/news/uk-22867315; **98** © 2015, Guardian News & Media Ltd.; **99** © 2014, Guardian News & Media Ltd.; **100** Der Tagesspiegel, 10.01.2013; **101** H. A. Harris in: Sport in Greece and Rome, Thames & Hudson, 1972; **101** Emil Zatopek; **101** Katherine Brown in: The Guardian, 25th December 2014; **103** © 2015, Guardian News & Media Ltd.; **105** © 2015, Guardian News & Media Ltd.; **106** TAZ, 24.03.2012; **107** Office for National Statistics, 2015; **107** Office for National Statistics; **107** Stephen Moss in: The Guardian, 28 April, 2015; **107** Clay Shirky in: wired.com, 2008, reprinted with permission of the author; **107** © 2015, Guardian News & Media Ltd.; **109** © 2015, Guardian News & Media Ltd.; **111** © 2015, Guardian News & Media Ltd.; **112** WDR, 25.07.2015; **113** Hilary Pilkington in: The Guardian, 20158; **113** © 2015, Guardian News & Media Ltd.; **113** Sir Andrew Green in: bbc.com/news, 2013; **113** Swaliha Bax in: The Guardian, 15th September 2015.

Sollte es in einem Einzelfall nicht gelungen sein, den korrekten Rechteinhaber ausfindig zu machen, so werden berechtigte Ansprüche selbstverständlich im Rahmen der üblichen Regelungen abgegolten.